HUG *Your* KIDS Today!

5 Key Lessons for Every Working Parent

8/20/08
Nicole,
Keep hugging!
Hugs matter!

MICHELLE NICHOLS

Good Friend Publishing
Reno, Nevada

To book Michelle Nichols to speak at your next meeting, conference, or event, call (877) 352-9684 toll-free or (775) 303-8201 direct.

For more information, visit www.HugYourKidsToday.com

Hug Your Kids Today! 5 Key Lessons for Every Working Parent

By Michelle Nichols

Printed in the United States of America

First Edition 2008

ISBN 978-0-9816567-2-4

This book may be ordered by mail from the publisher. Copies are available at special discounts for bulk purchases by corporations, institutions, and other organizations. To order one copy or thousands, please see the Quick Order Form at the back of the book or call the publisher, below.

Published by Good Friend Publishing. "A good book is a good friend."

P.O. Box 34090, Reno, Nevada, 89533 USA 775-303-8201

Designed by PonderosaPineDesign.com, Vicky Vaughn Shea

Cover photography by: ©iStockphoto.com/Miroslav Ferkuniak; ©iStockphoto.com/Michel de Nijs; ©iStockphoto.com/Lise Gagne; ©iStockphoto.com/Peter Zelei; Don Maynard; and Cassandra Hemsley.

NOTE: Due to privacy concerns, some dates and full names have been omitted.

Dedication

To God, the source of all love,

and to my family — Ron, Mark, Amy, and Devin.

Hugs for all!

I love all three of my kids, but there's one I especially wish I could hug right now — my oldest child, Kolleen, A.K.A. "KoRo." I can't because Kolleen died in a jet-skiing accident in May 2006, when she was 18. I still painfully miss her every day. Now the world, and our family, is short one talented, loving young woman.

Buy this book, read it and then go hug your kids. If you're married, hug your spouse too. Hugs matter!

—RALPH ROBERTS, Real estate entrepreneur and author of the best-selling book, *Flipping Houses for Dummies*

Whatever the question, let love be the answer.

— Dr. Wayne Dyer, American author

Love measures our stature; the more we love, the bigger we are.

— Rev. William Sloane Coffin, Jr. (1924 – 2006),

American peace activist

Preface

From Keynote to Love Note

I've been in the sales world for more than 25 years. From 2001 to 2007, I wrote 150 *Savvy Selling* columns and recorded 45 podcasts for *Business-Week.com*. I was also a professional speaker, offering keynote speeches and workshops. I've started four of my own companies and sold for five other organizations. I loved being in sales.

In the fall of 2007, I closed my company and prepared to do something different, but I wasn't sure what. I told my editors at *Business-Week.com* that I wasn't going to write for them anymore. I sent back the deposit checks for my upcoming speeches. Then I waited.

One evening, I thought: *The meaning of life is love.* I knew it was so important that I had to write it down. The next morning, reality set in. I'm a sales professional and now I'm supposed to write and speak about love? Like the movie *Titanic,* a basketful of puppies, or the song *Kumbaya?*

I felt like I'd accidentally opened someone else's mail. But no, this message was for me. So here's my family's love story — how we survived a tragedy together and our journey back to a meaningful life — and five key lessons for all working parents, which I learned along the way.

I hope this book will help you be a better mom, dad, stepparent, grandparent, employee, or employer. Enjoy!

Table of Contents

Introduction

What are your worst nightmares?

Until the middle of 1998, mine were being chased by a bad guy or going to work naked. However, in the last week of July that year, I had to do something more terrifying than anything I'd ever dreamed: I had to write the obituary for our eight and a half year old son, Mark. How do you sum up the life of your child?

But this book is not about nightmares. It's about life, hugs, and loving your kids. It's what I wish I'd known about parenting and working before Mark died. If you work and have children, I wrote it for you.

⋄○⋄

Working when you have children is like going to a high school dance. The band starts with a rock-and-roll song, you find your rhythm, and begin to dance. Then the next tune has a country-western beat and you have to find the new rhythm before you can dance again. Soon the band plays a slow song, and you need to find another rhythm before you can dance smoothly.

In the same way, the perfect plan for you and your kids that ran so smoothly yesterday may not work tomorrow, because the demands on your life keep changing. Maybe your son gets braces and now needs to go to the orthodontist twice a month. Or maybe your daughter starts to play the tuba and needs you to transport it to and from school every Thursday. Add in football games, piano recitals, and getting the dog fixed and, well — you get the picture.

In the midst of all this fancy footwork, your kids are growing up. No matter how busy you are dancing, you only have one chance to raise them. This book can help you make your one shot your *best* shot.

Wham! Bam! Damn!

I n the summer of 1998, Mark, his younger sister Amy, and Mark's buddy Billy attended a local day camp. Each morning, they would board a school bus to visit historical sites and go on nature hikes, and I'd pick them up in the afternoon. My husband had a job he enjoyed that paid enough to cover our bills. I was between jobs at the time. It was a working-class version of Camelot.

WHAM! Mark began vomiting one day a week, for three weeks in a row. At first, I thought it might be from eating bad mayonnaise in his lunches or riding on the bouncing buses. The doctors thought he just had the flu. But eleven days later, he died from brain cancer. Mark was bright, funny, and kind — and he never lived to start the fourth grade.

BAM! After Mark died, my parents abandoned us. They said to let them know when we were normal again.

During that first year, my mom called to announce, "We're off to Paris. Did you know it's been ten years since we've been to Paris?"

I wanted to tell her that no one in Paris had noticed.

Since they lived in California and we lived in Texas, I pleaded, "Can't you stop and see us on your way to Paris?"

"I'll tell you what," she replied. "I'll wave at you as we fly over your house."

DAMN! Two years later, our family decided to try to adopt a little boy. We met a three year old boy named Devin from Texas who needed a family but we quickly learned he wasn't legally available for adoption. We hired the best lawyers and started the adoption process anyway.

In the middle of the process, legal circumstances forced us to give him back to his birth mother. She didn't have any housing, transportation, or income. After our family had already buried our first son, we felt like we'd been asked to lay a second boy on the train tracks of life.

∽○∽

On the fifth anniversary of Mark's death, in July 2003, our family had two billboards put up along the major highways in Houston, Texas, just for one day. They said:

HUG YOUR KIDS TODAY. WE WISH WE COULD.
IN MEMORY OF MARK NICHOLS 1989–1998.

∽o∾

I don't tell you our story for sympathy. Rather, I want to show you that the five key lessons in this book were not just some good ideas I sat around and dreamed up. I learned them the hard way, from experience. I've looked back at these years to see what I did right and what I wish I'd done differently. Now I share my wisdom with you.

When You Lose, Don't Lose the Lesson Too

What did we learn from burying our first-born child, being abandoned by my parents, risking loving another child, and putting up billboards encouraging thousands of folks to hug their kids?

A lot. It is said that experience is a hard teacher because it gives the test first and the lesson afterward. I wrote this book so you could learn from our experiences.

Raising children is often a trial-and-error, do-it-yourself job. You frequently have to make instant decisions; only later do you know if they were the right choices. Most of us are better trained for our jobs than we are for parenting.

Here is our story. It's our journey to Hell and back, with twists and turns, villains and heroes. It even has a happy ending because eventually we were able to adopt Devin. Hooray!

A Disclaimer

You might suppose I'm a snuggly, huggy-type of person. On the contrary, my voice can be like an army drill sergeant's. My point-of-view is often, "Buck up, life is hard." Patience is not one of my best qualities. I'm embarrassed to admit that I once yelled at Mark when we were playing Candy Land because he didn't move his marker quickly enough.

I once wanted to be an efficiency expert. I am also very practical. Years ago, I was in a business partnership called *Intensely Practical*. My challenge is that love is neither efficient nor intensely practical.

∾o∾

I wish I could tell you that I'm a leading authority on love or that I were the love equivalent of Bill Gates or Warren Buffett, giving away billions of units of love rather than billions of dollars.

The truth is I'm none of those things — but I have had some moments of brilliant love. Perhaps that is enough. Although I'm not a love expert, I hope to be one of its top salespeople.

And I'm Mark's mom. As you read our story and ponder my five key lessons, I hope that at some point, a light will go on inside of your heart. Or maybe you'll hear a click in your head, or you'll feel like a key has unlocked something inside of you, and you'll think, "Aha!"

∾o∾

In Chapter One, "What's so Hard about Working When You Have Kids?" you can identify which aspects of being a working parent are most challenging for you.

In Chapter Two, "Mark's Story," you can learn a bit about Mark's life. In Chapter Three, "Restarting Our Hearts," you can read about our first years of grief and the start of our journey back to happiness.

In Chapter Four, "The Lesson is Love," you can explore the foundational idea for this book — love.

In Chapters Five through Nine, you'll find my five key lessons — "Hug Your Kids Today," *"Carpe Kids,"* "When All Else Fails, Laugh," "Develop Your Family's Faith Life," and "Hug Your Kids Every Day."

After each lesson, I asked six successful working parents to share a nugget of their experience and wisdom. I call these "Hugs from Michelle's Friends."

In Chapter Ten, "Go Forth and Love Abundantly," you are encouraged to turn these ideas into action.

I hope this book helps you feel more love with your family, happiness at work, and peace in your life.

PART 1

Life's Toughest Teacher: Experience

*What the world really needs is more love
and less paperwork.*

⁓Pearl Bailey (1918 – 1990), American singer

CHAPTER 1

Prescription without diagnosis is malpractice.
—Medical rule-of-thumb

If it's neither snow nor rain nor heat nor gloom of night, what the devil is wrong with the place?
—Anthony M. Frank, former Postmaster General

What's so Hard about Working When You Have Kids?

In 2006, there were more than 50 million working moms and dads in America with children under the age of 18, according to the U.S. Bureau of Labor Statistics. So, what's so hard about working when you're a parent? To borrow a phrase from poet Elizabeth Barrett Browning, "Let me count the ways."

My research uncovered more than 150 concerns of working parents. They basically break down into "Shoulds" and "Wants."

Which of these are most challenging for you?

- ❏ I should work long hours for success at work.
- ❏ I should raise healthy and well-adjusted kids.
- ❏ I should have a good relationship with my spouse.
- ❏ I should provide for my family's needs.
- ❏ I should respond to the requests of my boss, customers, and co-workers.
- ❏ I should maintain a well-run and clean home.
- ❏ I should ensure that everyone in my family eats nutritionally, exercises regularly, gets enough sleep, has clean clothes, maintains their health, goes to religious services, and develops outside interests.
- ❏ I should pay my bills on time and manage my investments.
- ❏ I should volunteer for the PTA and other worthy causes.
- ❏ I want to have fun.
- ❏ I want to earn the money, promotions, prestige and kudos of a successful career.
- ❏ I want my kids and spouse to love me and to know I love them, too.
- ❏ I want the respect of my family, company, and community.
- ❏ I want to enjoy my extended family and friends.
- ❏ I want to have time for my hobbies and interests.
- ❏ I want to relax and enjoy all I worked so hard to achieve.

The Good News about Work

Work has a mere four letters but it's a big deal in our adult lives. It provides:

Money – Duh!

Financial benefits – Work can provide medical insurance, retirement programs, and disability and life insurance. You probably also receive paid holidays and vacations.

Perks – Perhaps you receive occasional baseball tickets, a chance to win a trip to Hawaii or an audience with a famous person through your work.

Satisfaction – Despite all the griping about work, you feel satisfaction when you accomplish a task, whether it's creating a product, completing a report, or leading a team to be injury-free for a year.

A place to compete – If you played sports growing up, you probably enjoy the competitive aspects of work: winning, keeping score, and ranking who sold the most or had the most billable hours.

A feeling of belonging to a team – For example, perhaps you're "on the sales team for Territory X" or "on the legal team serving Client A."

Opportunities for a leadership role – At work, you can get promotions. As you rise up the ranks, you can lead others.

An outlet for creativity – There is a creative aspect to all jobs, not just those in the arts or design fields. You can use your creativity in writing a winning sales proposal or constructing a successful medical solution.

Identity and status – "What do you do?" is the most common opening question at social or networking events. (Thankfully, "What's your sign?" has run its course.) Your work is part of your identity. If you're like most workers, being able to tell yourself and others, "I am a C.P.A." or "I am a business executive" is important to you.

It's no wonder work is so important to us!

The Seduction of Work

Work can be like the devil. I once heard a pastor say that the devil befriends you quickly and corrupts you slowly. If you routinely go home from work at 5:30 p.m. until one week, when you're working on a big project and don't leave until 6:00 each night, it may be no big deal. It's just an extra half-hour per day. You notice that your children and your spouse don't crumble. Then soon, you begin leaving work at 6:00 p.m. every day — until 6:00 p.m. becomes 6:30, which then becomes 7:00 and then 7:30 and so on.

∽o∽

One of the biggest challenges of work is that there is no standard conversion rate and the rewards from work and family are so different.

For example, if your employer paid you in yen but you wanted to buy something in dollars, there is a standard conversion rate between the currencies. However, there is no rate to convert an hour spent gaining a new client or preparing an expansion plan to an hour spent with your family.

As to the different rewards, for most of us, the financial benefits of work are:

Measurable – X dollars or pounds or yen

Routine – paid on a regular schedule

Consistent – you get paid the same amount or according to the same pay plan on a routine basis until something changes

Immediate – after you work a few weeks, you get paid

Subject to regularly scheduled increases – based upon quarterly or annual reviews

In addition, when you do a good job, you might receive a trophy, gift, or a pat on the back.

Yet none of the rules for the rewards of work apply to your family. The love you get from your family is not measurable, routine, consistent, immediate, or subject to regularly scheduled increases.

In fact, it's not uncommon for there to be a very long delay — maybe even 25 or 35 years — before you are rewarded for your love by your children. Of course, sometimes you get rewarded by your family right away, with a squeeze, a "Gee thanks, Dad," or a peanut-buttery kiss.

SUMMARY

Working when you have kids is hard because there are so many "Shoulds" and "Wants" competing for your time and energy. Work has many benefits, but it can also be seductive. There is no conversion rate between an hour spent at work and one spent with your family.

CHAPTER 2

Tell a joke, share and be a good friend.

—What Mark Nichols, age 8½, said his life stood for, in his last conversation

There is a land of the living and a land of the dead and the bridge is love.

—Thornton Wilder (1897–1975) American playwright

Mark's self-portrait, age 8

Mark's Story

"It's a boy!" the doctors announced to my husband, Ron, and me one day in October 1989. The baby was our first-born child, and we named him Mark.

Becoming parents was wonderful. It was as if our world went from black and white to color.

Despite our typical first-time parents' clumsiness, Mark grew up just fine. He was everything a parent dreams of — cute, healthy, kind, and smart.

I was a very protective mom. I changed the words to the song "Three Blind Mice" because I thought the original was too violent. My kids were in elementary school before they discovered that their version was different from the standard. Here's how I taught it to them:

Three blind mice. Three blind mice.

See how they run. See how they run.

They all ran after the farmer's wife.

Who kissed them all and made them sandwiches.

Did you ever see such a sight in your life

As three blind mice.

Reading buddies. Mark, age 2, "reads" Babar to his stuffed elephants.

On the Move

efore Mark was two years old, we moved to Houston, Texas, where our daughter, Amy was born. Our family was now complete; we had a boy, a girl, a house, and two dogs.

When Mark was six years old, we moved to Austin, Texas. He attended a small, country school called Dominican Academy, run by a pair of elderly nuns, Sisters Benita and Leona.

The parents were all frightened by the nuns, but the kids loved them. Sister Benita had a dirt collection — little vials of earth that people had brought her from all over the world and even from the moon.

When Mark met Sister Leona, his kindergarten teacher, she asked him how he got to the school. He told her his address and every right and left turn we took to get to the distant school. She listened patiently. At the end, she told me that most kids just told her they got to the school in their car.

After Mark was in kindergarten for ten days, he was promoted to first grade.

Life with Mark

ven though his intellect was years ahead of his age, in many ways, Mark was a typical little boy. He loved building with Legos, riding his bike, and participating in Cub Scout events. He liked playing Nintendo with his friends and watching action movies like James Bond and Star Wars. He was very social; he always wanted to have a friend over or to be over at a friend's home. He liked to organize and give parties. He had a Clue party, and a Super Bowl party, too.

Mark played Little League baseball, soccer, and basketball. He was not a gifted athlete; I purposely kept him in sports so he'd develop respect for other kids' talents. It also helped some of his friends to accept Mark's intelligence when they saw him struggle at moves that came naturally to them on the fields or courts.

Mark was fun to be around. According to one of his friends, "He was a very funny boy and he knew at least 200 funny jokes. He was a good friend." Mark liked to make up jokes and he liked to entertain us at family parties by telling us jokes. Here's one of his originals: What do you call a girl with bad breath? Halle Tosis.

Mark was also known for his kindness. As one of his teachers commented, "My fondest memory of Mark is not his intellect or sense of humor but his GREAT BIG SMILE!" His 94 year old great-grandfather wrote me a note that read, "I appreciate that Mark had the time to sit down and play checkers with me." When Mark played sports, he couldn't bring himself to steal the ball from other players. If someone on the other team fell down, he'd run over and help them up. I always pictured him as the team chaplain.

One time, he asked me for a shoebox. I didn't think to ask him why, but later found the note Mark put inside it, written to Jim Thome, MVP for the Cleveland Indians that year (1998):

Dear Mr. Thome, I love your hitting. I am a big fan. Can you send me an autographed baseball, picture and card? Your best fan, Mark Nichols P.S. I have enclosed an autographed baseball by me.

We are family. Ron, Amy, Mark, and Michelle on a family hike in the Sierra Nevada, the summer before Mark died.

We never sent the note and ball, and now they're treasured possessions.

Soon after Mark started second grade, we moved to Reno, Nevada. We worked hard to buy a home zoned for Roy Gomm Elementary because it was a small school with a long reputation for providing a great education. The only thing Mark didn't like was the school's mascot — a gopher! Their motto was to "Go-Fer Excellence" (groan).

By the time Mark was eight years old, he'd had a total of six addresses in three states. Later, Mark told me that going to Heaven would be like one more move for him.

But I'm jumping ahead.

Mark's Last Month

As I mentioned earlier, in the summer of 1998, Mark was eight and a half years old, and his sister, Amy, was six and a half years old. Amy, Mark, and his friend Billy went to a local summer day camp.

Schoolteachers ran the camp and they had the students keep daily diaries. Every day, Mark recorded their activities, Amy's behavior, and added, "I miss Mom." When I asked him if he was too old to be missing his mom, he just shrugged. He wasn't embarrassed at all.

Toward the end of camp, for three weeks in a row, Mark threw up one day a week. Then Mark became sick for several consecutive days, so we took him to a pediatrician. After running some blood tests, which all came back fine, the doctor suggested an MRI.

"An MRI for occasional barfing?" I told the doctor. The MRI revealed that Mark had a tumor on his brain stem. Our whole family felt like we'd been sucker-punched.

Mark spent the next two days in the hospital receiving fluids and steroids. When they released him, he went swimming that afternoon. The next day, Mark and Billy went to their buddy Luke's house and they built model cars. For lunch, they each ate a whole box of macaroni and cheese.

Then Luke and Billy walked Mark back to our house, so we could drive to Sacramento, two hours away. We needed to meet his brain

Mark's send-off. Luke Mudge (left) and Billy Vicks (right) send off Mark (center) to his brain surgery.

surgeon before Mark's surgery, which was scheduled for the next morning. The three boys posed for photos — making silly faces as only little boys can do. These photos, and their memories, turned out to be their parting gifts to Mark.

We Meet the "C Word"

M ark was scheduled for brain surgery the next morning. The doctors planned to cut a square out of his skull, take out the tumor, then put back the square. We teased Mark that we hoped they'd put the square back in the right way.

My parents lived about two hours away from the hospital. My mom came and sat with us during his operation.

After Mark's surgery, his brain surgeon told us his results. "Good news, Mr. and Mrs. Nichols — we got the tumor out. Bad news — it's cancer and it's already spread to a spot that's too dangerous for surgery. It's stage 4." We later learned that cancer is graded in four stages, with "4" being the most advanced.

Up until this time, everyone had used the word "tumor." This was the first time they'd used the hammer word "cancer." It hit us hard.

Three days later, on a Friday, we met with his oncologists for the first time. They gave Mark a 50/50 chance of surviving for five years. I was really upset that he might not live to be 13½ years old. That afternoon, Luke's mother came and picked up Amy to bring her back to their home so Ron and I could concentrate on Mark's recovery.

The following night, Mark suddenly started screaming in pain. In hospitals, they ask patients to grade their pain on a scale of 1–10. Mark was usually about a 3–5, so when he started yelling, "I'm a 10, I'm a 10," we all knew something was very wrong. Within half an hour, the pain was so great that he had a seizure and stopped breathing.

They put him on a ventilator. His heart continued to beat just fine. The next day, the doctors did a test to see if any blood was getting to his brain. I prayed, "Dear God. You haven't answered any of my prayers so far, but I'm begging you, either give him a 90% or more or a 0%. Please don't give us a 50%."

My prayer was answered, but not in the way I'd hoped. Mark wasn't getting any blood to his brain. Although it was terrible news, it was definitive.

Mark's Peace Bear and Last Wishes

n Mark's last days with us, two cool things happened.

Like most moms and dads, when my children are sick I'll do anything to cheer them up. As Mark tried to recover from his brain surgery, I asked him if there was anything I could get him to make him feel better. I mentioned Beanie Babies. He held up two fingers. At that time, these little stuffed animals were selling for about $30 apiece.

"Two? You want two Beanies?" I asked. I thought that was rather greedy, which was unlike Mark.

He shook his head, "No."

I bent down and he whispered in my ear, "Peace." He didn't want two; he was making the peace sign.

My sister tracked down a Peace Bear Beanie Baby, never realizing the deeper significance of a little boy asking for peace just before he was to pass over. That stuffed animal now sits in front of his ashes, a prized memento and a lesson for us all.

∽๏∾

Just before Mark died, I was able to ask him all my big questions.

Here are some of them and Mark's answers. My explanatory comments are in parentheses. I also asked him some curve-ball questions, like "What colors should I paint the house?" and "Explain thermodynamics," which he politely ignored.

Why do you have to go now?
I was supposed to be like a shooting star or a meteor, shining brightly for a short time.

Explain life.
Everyone's life has a path. This is mine. Grandpa J's is to be 93 years old, have two different kinds of cancer, and golf on! You've got to follow your path and let me follow mine.

But we'll miss you.
Only physically. But it will teach you to look harder for me everywhere. I am a big hug of love around all those who loved me.

How will I know when you're around?
I am *always* with you. Like love, like God. I will be in memories of us that crack you up or guide you. And I will leave lots of little signs.

Mark, how will we get through our grief over losing you?
First of all, I'll never be out of your spirit-lives or memories. In other words, now no matter where you go, I am with you!

And you have to respect me and allow me to follow my path. We each have a path. I feel I crammed a lot more than eight and a half years of living in my life and whenever anyone else faces death, they can be comforted knowing I have gone ahead.

I know I'll be playing Nintendo in Heaven, but at first I'll just lie on a pillow in the lap of Jesus. I have tried to be a good Christian — but I still don't think I could sing the song of the books of the Bible without the list! (His Sunday school class had been practicing this song.)

Anyway, I know Mom is comforted knowing my soul is in Heaven and my spirit is all around, especially telling jokes, sharing and being a great friend. That's what I hope my life has stood for.

Organ donation?
To the extreme. Share!

Mark, Dad feels guilty that he didn't want kids until he held you.
Forgive yourself, Dad. You are being entirely too hard on yourself. Maybe kids to you are like pistachio ice cream. Green and chunky ice cream? It looks and sounds weird! But you tried fatherhood and were big enough to do it right, do it big, and love the job.

I know you love being my Dad because I heard all your gears grinding on how to accommodate my cancer treatments. You were willing to be a contortionist in your life just for me — that's love in action.

Dad, you were a great dad. A 100%, not 99%, dad. I am very proud of you. I really liked how you gave so much of your time and energy to be the coach of my baseball team.

I really appreciate all the money and time you spent on educational stuff. You put your love for me into action and that makes me feel really special.

I'm looking forward to you sending me off on a cloud of love. I have to leave. My whole body is flying apart. You can't keep me here.

How did you learn to love so much?
Easy. My whole family really, truly, deeply loves each other. They say you learn what you live. Well, wherever we lived, and we lived all over, we had each other and we really loved each other.

∞○∞

On Mark's last day, about a dozen family members including my mom and dad, brother and sister, mother-in-law, and Mark's godparents, gathered around him and told him goodbye. Around noon, the doctors repeated their tests and confirmed he'd been brain dead for more than a day. Ron and I said our last goodbyes to Mark before they turned off his ventilator. His life journey was over.

Cremation and Cookies

Ron and I drove from the hospital to a nearby crematory to make Mark's arrangements. To make matters more difficult, the saleslady put the hard sell on us.

It was a long drive home. We were in shock. Our pastor was scheduled to come to our home that evening and I felt convinced that I needed to make homemade cookies for him. We'd never had a pastor come to our home and I was sure that store-bought ones would not do. Thankfully, I found a box of brownie mix and made them.

∞○∞

When we got to Luke's home to pick up Amy, naturally her first questions concerned her brother. "Where's Mark?" Was he in the car? Was he still in the hospital? We stalled her until we got home.

When we stepped inside our front door, Ron told her Mark had died. A wail started in her toes, charged up her six year old body, and roared out her mouth. She spoke for our whole family.

∞○∞

Our pastor came to our home that night. I'm sure he didn't even notice that the cookies were homemade. He tried to comfort us but we were emotionally out of reach.

The day eventually ended and we went to bed.

CHAPTER 3

When you're going through Hell, keep going.
⇒Prime Minister Winston Churchill (1874–1965)

True love stories never have endings.
⇒Richard Bach, American author

Love begins at home.
⇒Mother Teresa (1910 – 1997), Founder of the Missionaries of Charity

Restarting Our Hearts

As anyone who's been through the death of a loved one knows, it feels like time should stop while you catch your breath, but actually, it's a blessing that time rolls on. Prime Minister Churchill was right: if you get sent to Hell, start marching out, however slowly.

What's unique about when a child dies is it's not a "circle of life" type of event. Our DNA is programmed, at the cellular level, to expect to bury our grandparents and parents. Logically speaking, we have about a 50/50 chance of having our siblings, best friends and even spouses die before we do.

However, when a child dies, it shakes us to the center of our souls because it violates the natural order. After all, our children are supposed to bury us and write our obituaries, not the other way around.

Here's our story of how we walked out, restarted our hearts, and created new lives.

MARK NICHOLS

On a Monday in July 1998, our dear son and friend, Mark Nichols, died after brain surgery. Your love and prayers while he tried to recover gave him great comfort.

He crammed a lot of living into his eight and a half years. Born in October 1989 in the Bay Area of California, he also lived in Houston and Austin, Texas, before moving to Reno, Nevada, almost two years ago.

Mark was a straight-A student at Roy Gomm Elementary, a Cub Scout in Den 10/Pack 53, and a member of Good Shepherd church. He played on various soccer, basketball, and baseball teams. Mark's advice in life was to, "Tell a joke, share, and be a good friend."

Please do not send flowers. There is a wonderful camp for children with cancer, their siblings and families. Please direct your donations to: Camp Okizu, 16 Digital Drive Novato, CA 94949.

A "Celebration of Life" for Mark will be held on (details.)

The love and support of our friends (and Mark's friends) have helped us get through this difficult time. Thank you for all you have done for us.

Ron, Michelle, and Amy Nichols

Mark's Celebration of Life

bout two weeks after Mark died, we had his "Celebration of Life." At the service, Ron and I spoke about Mark and our love for him. Per Mark's request, we collected stories from the attendees and had a "make your own ice cream sundae" party afterwards.

I wrote in his Celebration program: *Through all the tears, the sadness and the pain comes the one thought that can get me through: I loved Mark and he loved me. Mark was my friend and I was his friend. Mark made me laugh and I made him laugh. We shared a slice of life together.*

One boy brought a jar with four pollywogs to the Celebration. He explained he'd always promised Mark he'd bring him some pollywogs but he never did — until now. What a reminder that you don't always have tomorrow to do a favor for your friends or loved ones.

Can You Lose Your Child Without Losing Your Mind?

know it's common to step around the word "died" and use phrases like "lost." I agree with grief specialist Darcie Sims, PhD, and I always say Mark *died* because I didn't lose him. I've lost my car keys before. If I look hard, I can find them and life will return to normal. That was not the case with Mark.

༺∞༻

Three days after Mark died, I began to write in a journal. The rest of this chapter has excerpts from the many journals I wrote in during my first few years of grief. When people say, "I can't imagine what it's like to have a child die," here's how it was for us.

༺∞༻

Excerpts From My Journals

On the outside, people seem to think about me, "She looks so together. She has handled Mark's death really well. I would fall apart. I don't know how she does it. It must be awful. But she keeps on. She is coming through remarkably well."

But on the inside, I'm thinking, "What happened? How do I back up, get you back in my life and then drive forward?" My life doesn't make sense to me right now.

∾∞∾

According to experts, there are five stages of grief — denial, anger, bargaining, depression, and acceptance — but I say there is only one stage: It hurts!

I am trying to let in the idea that you are dead, but I get so upset I have to slam the door shut. It's those peeks into the future that really hurt. I can deal with you not being here today. It's the idea of you not being here for the rest of my life that shakes me to my core; it is unspeakable.

Yesterday, Luke wanted to show his mom how he could talk like a vampire. She told him, "Go away and stop interrupting me."

Mark, I wish you could interrupt me to talk like a vampire.

∾∞∾

Today I heard the fourth graders playing their recorders and I got so sad that you never really learned how to play yours. The only song you knew was "Hot Cross Buns." Then I thought about all the unsung music in your life and I felt *really* sad.

Ron's Grief Walk

Ron keeps saying, "I need Mark here with me." He repeats it so often, it's like he's hallucinating!

Mark is fine on his own. He can wait until Ron's natural death to be together again. Mark doesn't reciprocate Ron's longing to be together. Somehow, I know that Ron has to let Mark go to get him back in his heart. I feel Mark wants to tell Ron, "Live until you die, Dad."

∾∞∾

Sometimes Everything is Still Not Enough

by Michelle Nichols 1999

The doctors said to us,
We did all that we could.
We pulled out all the stops.
Cost was no issue.
Time spent was not a problem.
We consulted every specialist.
But despite all our efforts,
both the heroic and the mundane,
he's dead.
And now there is nothing more we can do for Mark.
We tried everything we could think of
but we couldn't save him.
Sometimes everything is still not enough.

So I wrote down every memory of him.
I looked at every photo and videotape.
I stuffed my brain with him.
I tried to console myself with how proud
he made his dad and me.
I tried to think how bad the cancer could
have tormented him and for how long,
before he finally lost his fight.
I tried to accept that his death was not an accident
because his birth and life were surely not an accident.
I did everything I could think of
but I couldn't heal my heart.
Sometimes everything is still not enough.

Ron wrote in a card to me "Mark will always occupy a special place in our hearts and I only wish there was some magic pill to make the hurt go away. I would give anything to go back in time and I know you would, too."

‿◦‿

Mark, Dad is still so wiped out from your death. He told his doctor that when he served in Vietnam and his unit was ambushed, he went in and saved his buddies – but he couldn't save you. He felt so helpless!

Our First Holidays Sans Mark

Thanksgiving

I've been wondering, what on earth do I have to be thankful for since your death? And the answer is – your life!

Grandma E said on your last day, how grateful we are that we got eight and a half great years – your whole life! – with us.

Mark's ornaments. Amy and I hand-painted 170 Christmas ornaments, about 5 inches across, similar to this one. Our friends helped us too. We gave them to friends of Mark and our family.

Christmas, from my journal

As Christmas approaches, I am determined that the Grinch that stole you, i.e. the cancer, is not going to steal my Christmas. I will fix my heart on the gift of the birth of life-changing babies – you *and* Jesus.

From our Christmas letter

How are we doing? We loved Mark, therefore we grieve. But we live because we are alive. There is no other choice. Having a child or friend die is the worst thing that can happen. Thank you for all your prayers, calls, hugs, and cards of support. We appreciate each one.

What can we learn from Mark's sudden death? To have fun *today*. To tell the people you care about that they are special *today*. To be kind and generous to everyone *today*.

How do we get through this tough time? All we can say is, "True love never dies."

Mother's Day

Mother's Day was really hard for me today. I bawled my head off. Then just as I was going to sleep, I came across this Bible verse: "As a mother comforts her child, so I will comfort you" (*Isaiah 66:13*). Afterward, I slept soundly.

Moving from Mark's House

About eight months after Mark died, we moved from Reno to Houston for a good job for Ron. The week before we moved, we dedicated two benches at his elementary school, which were donated by the parent-faculty association and his Cub Scout pack. We distributed his books, "A Celebration of Mark's Life," just as he requested, with more than 150 recollections.

The newspaper sent a photographer and a journalist. The next day's article was glorious. "They came to remember, honor Mark," the title said, with a big color picture and a full-page story.

Having the movers pack up his room was tough. Even tougher was when the movers at the new house showed me the boxes labeled "Mark's Room" and asked me, "Where is Mark's room?" – and there wasn't one.

An Uninvited Monster Moves In
By Michelle Nichols 1999

The day my son Mark died, a big, ugly monster moved into our home. We don't like it one bit. He was not invited. We never even met him before; he just showed up and now he won't leave. He gets in the way of everything we do.

Since he looks like he's here for a long stay, we have just learned to work around him. We vacuum and dust around him. When we have gatherings, he just sits there, in the middle of the couch. He doesn't say much; he doesn't have to. Just his presence is enough to put a damper on our lives.

His name is Grief.

We wish he'd never come. We hate having him here in our home. At first, we dropped subtle hints that we wanted Grief to go away. Then our voices got louder and our pleas became direct orders. He just ignored us.

Sometimes Grief goes away for short periods but he always comes back. It is almost worse than before he left, because we had hoped that this time he was gone for good. He's like a boomerang.

When he wouldn't leave us, we tried to leave him. We went away on vacation but Grief came along too. We even moved to another state but that didn't work either. He was waiting for us on the doorstep when we arrived and moved into that home with us, too.

We hope someday he'll move out permanently. Maybe it will be lonely, though, because we won't have our dear Mark and we also won't have Grief to at least take up some space and attention.

Maybe Grief can stay a while longer.

Grief, the Day Mark Died.
Art by Amy Nichols, age 7

I'm Still Standing — Mark's First Anniversary

Today is a major milestone for our family. Mark you left us one year ago. We have had a few deeply sad moments today but we also had some good laughs and enjoyed the beauty of Lake Tahoe.

We are so grateful for the steady love, support, and comfort you and God have supplied throughout this year.

~o~

For our second Christmas without Mark, Ron and I each wrote a long letter to him. Here are two excerpts.

From Ron

In this time of reflection, we are reminded of how much we miss you and how much we love you. We are still grieving, Mark — perhaps more this year than last. At times, it seems I remember every detail, and other times I can't remember a thing.

But what is constant is that your life stood for all the right things. Mark, you are a kind, gentle, decent human being. It has nothing to do with how smart you were, but has everything to do with how big a heart you had. Son, as a person you stood tall, and that really is the measure of a man.

Every day I am reminded of how important you were to me and how sad I am now that you're gone. But in our family reflections we always talk about what a kind person you were. Those are the memories we cherish.

I wish I could say we are getting through the ordeal of your death but the truth is we are devastated. I still cry every day and mourn what could have been. What should have been.

One thing that will never change though: How proud I am to have you as a son and to be your dad. I look toward the heavens, hoping to see you and hoping you are looking down on us. No matter where you are, you will always be part of the family — a family that loves you very much, a family that misses you terribly.

My heart still has a big hole in it, but it's a hole that will be mended once we are together again.

I love you son. DAD

From Michelle

You know my heart is broken, but it's healing into a new shape. It's like if I broke my leg but I didn't get a cast and I just sort of hopped and wobbled along until it healed. I will have to walk on that misshapen leg the rest of my life. By choice, I will not sit in my chair and do nothing. I choose to reach out, speak about you and our love, demonstrate gentleness and love, and learn more about the human experience.

I miss you hugely. I miss ruffling your hair, touching you, and hugging you. I miss your radiant smile A LOT. I wonder what other party plans you had in you when you died – or did you just hold them in Heaven?

I am thankful for your many gifts, but it is your kindness that I am most proud of.

I love you, Mark! Love Forever, Mom.

Billboards of Love

On the fifth anniversary of Mark's death, our family had two identical billboards put up along the major highways, just for one day, in Houston, Texas. An estimated 550,000 people saw the billboards. Several thousand more people saw them when KTRK, the ABC-TV affiliate in Houston, ran a beautiful interview of our family and a story about the billboards on their two evening newscasts. You can watch the TV clip on www.HugYourKidsToday.com.

The billboard that led to this book. Houston billboard in July 2003.

Billboard #2. Billboard design for July 21, 2008. Artwork courtesy of Clear Channel Outdoor

To honor Mark's tenth anniversary, we started National Hug Your Kids Day. The purpose is to remind parents to stop and hug their kids. The first celebration will be held July 21, 2008. The holiday will be celebrated on the third Monday of each July every year thereafter.

In 2008, we'll have nationwide digital billboards, a custom song, and YouTube videos. Clear Channel Outdoor will donate space on many of their digital billboards across the United States. They will all carry the same message on the same day. WOW!

Songwriter and performer Tony Brigmon wrote and recorded a custom song for the project, called, "Hug Your Kids Today." You can download it for free from the web site. It's a great song to play when you're hugging your kids or dancing.

There are many touching and funny YouTube videos created with this song on the web site. Perhaps you will want to make one too. We will have a contest for the best YouTube video each month.

We are looking at setting the Guinness World Record for the largest number of parents hugging their kids at one time. Maybe you can join us!

To see the YouTube videos, download the song, or learn more about the project, go to www.HugYourKidsToday.com

Faith, hope and love. But the greatest of these is love.
— The Bible (1 Cor 13:13)

CHAPTER 4

No three words have greater power than "I love You."
—Unknown

To love someone deeply gives you strength.
Being loved by someone deeply gives you courage.
—Lao Tzu (approx. 600–300 B.C.), father of Taoism

The Lesson is Love

To paraphrase a famous saying, "What doesn't kill me makes me stronger — and wiser." My parents only came to visit us once in the first year and a half after Mark died. They rarely called. They sent Hallmark cards but even when you "care enough to send the very best," the cards fell far short of what we needed. I felt like I was on a battlefield and two of my key soldiers had suddenly run away.

As you've probably experienced, family relationships are magnified. Your relatives can make you happier, or hurt you deeper, than those outside your blood-and-marriage circle. Parents and children seem to have the highest expectations of each other, and therefore, the highest opportunities to love or wound each other.

Before Mark died, my parents had been typical Ward-and-June-Cleaver-type parents to me and traditional grandparents to Mark and Amy. Their behavior especially hurt Amy, who was their only remaining grandchild at the time and, to this day, their only granddaughter. She needed their support at least as much as I did. The details would make you cry.

I won't lie. I felt hurt, mad, and sad — sometimes all at once, like a stew of pain. I tried arguing with them, pleading with them and ignoring them, but nothing worked. I just hurt more and more, and they ran farther and farther away from us until soon, they were only a speck on our horizon. They stayed away from us for many years. To this day, I cannot understand their behavior.

On the first anniversary of Mark's death, Amy and I went to their home to tell them how we felt. "You broke my heart," I began. My parents calmly but firmly told me, they wanted me to stew. They said they wanted to teach me a lesson.

∽o∽

You're probably wondering, "What lesson did they have in mind?"

I have no idea. However, during our years of healing, I learned a lesson that changed the rest of my life. The lesson is love.

What is Love?

Love is a serious mental disease.
Plato (424 BC–348 BC), Greek philosopher

Where there is love there is life.
Mahatma Gandhi (1869–1948), Indian philosopher

Love is what makes you smile when you're tired.
Chrissy, age 6

Love is like good art; you know it when you see it, or experience it. Even billionaire investor Warren Buffett has weighed in on love. In 2007, according to an interview in the *Harvard Crimson*, he told 98 Harvard students, "Unconditional love is the most powerful force in the universe. I got unconditional love from my parents."

Dr. Martin Luther King, Jr. saw love as more powerful than violence. He used love to fight discrimination and advocate for civil rights. He said, "Hate cannot drive out hate: only love can do that."

Legacy Loving

Dying is easy. Living is hard.
Dr. Wilson (played by Robert Sean Leonard) on the FOX-TV show, *House.*

*Let us live so that when we come to die even the undertaker
will be sorry.*
Mark Twain (1835–1910), American humorist

*What's the difference between death and taxes?
You can only get an extension on your taxes.*
Classic CPA joke

I was leading a CEO workshop recently, and as the participants introduced themselves, one man crowed, "I'm a first-time dad! My wife just delivered our son at 2:00 a.m. this morning." He was probably thinking how dedicated he was, but all I could think was, "How sad."

This was the inaugural day for his new family, and instead of staying with them to bask in the wonder of it all, he was at work. He probably assumed, as many people do, that he had plenty of tomorrows to spend time with his new child.

∽◦∾

Writing Mark's obituary naturally led me to think about my own obituary. What would my family write if I died today? And more importantly, what would I want it to say?

What do you want yours to say? According to Steven Covey's landmark book, *The 7 Habits of Highly Effective People*, habit #2 is "to begin with the end in mind."

Imagine yourself at the end of your life. How do you want to be remembered? As a leader in your field? Perhaps the CEO of a major corporation? That's great — but if you died today, how would your children remember you? If they're young, they probably won't be impressed with your career accomplishments. Their best memories will be of the times you spent throwing a ball with them or helping them finish their science fair projects. Kids remember love in action.

Your customers and companies rely on you to supply them with goods and services to keep their businesses rolling along. The bitter truth is, if you weren't there, they could probably get their problems solved some other way.

Your family relies on you much more than all of your customers and co-workers combined. To your children, spouse, and other loved ones, there is only one you. You cannot be replaced, and there is no substitute for you loving and hugging them.

∽o∾

I decided I wanted my obituary and tombstone to say:

She loved a lot.

I don't want it to say "She worked a lot" or "She sold a lot." Besides, I can show my love to my customers or company in the way I work with them. However, my work is only a subset of who I am. My life's goal is now to love a lot.

∽o∾

Big corporations have mission statements, vision statements, and values statements.

Here are my mission statement, vision statement, and values statement all rolled together: Love.

What are yours?

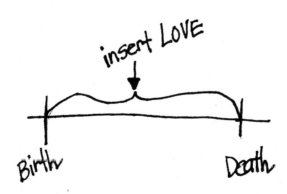

Between Life and Death, Insert Love.

Finding More Time to Love Your Loved Ones

It's not enough to be busy, so are the ants. The question is, what are we busy about?

Henry David Thoreau (1817–1862), American writer

You have a lifetime to work, but children are only young once.

Polish Proverb

P icture a hamster on a wheel. The hamster is running its little hamster heart out on that wheel, but soon it is very tired — and it hasn't really achieved anything.

Will running faster help? No.

Will running at certain days or times help? Obviously not.

Will wearing expensive hamster running shoes help? No, again.

Now imagine this hamster is wearing a business suit with a Blackberry hanging off its belt. Does it remind you of anyone?

Whenever I talk to working parents, they almost always tell me they are stressed and exhausted. I bet if I could interview this hamster it would feel the same way.

Running hard all day, every day, not only makes you tired, it lowers your productivity, health, and happiness. You also lose opportunities to have more pleasure, fun and laughs with your family. After all, what is the point of life if you don't have fun with the people you care about?

～○～

Step One to finding more time for our loved ones is to forget "work-life balance." It is the wrong goal and a road to insanity.

There are two problems with the idea of trying to balance your work and family. One, the word "balance" implies that the two elements are of equal importance. They're not. Work is your livelihood; your family is your life. If you lose your job, you can get another one. If you lose a child, you cannot replace him or her.

The second problem is, since you only have 24 hours in a day, you can't keep adding to both sides of the scale. If you are already doing 25 things for work and 25 things for your family, you can't add 3 more to both sides, even if you would theoretically stay in balance.

This is where many working parents get themselves into trouble. For example, if you are already running a full schedule of work and family, and the boss asks you to take over another project for the next six months, you might be tempted to justify it by also taking on coaching your child's sports team. On paper, you are still in balance. In reality, you're over-committed.

Prioritize Your Family First and Work a Close Second

Housework can kill you if done right.
Erma Bombeck (1927–1996), American humorist

I don't even butter my bread. I consider that cooking.
Katherine Cebrian, American author

S tep Two is to prioritize and put "spending some quality time with your family" as your top priority every day. Even if it's just time for a good hug before you start your day, it will pay benefits all day long.

This simple plan works because whatever is #1 on your "to-do" list probably gets done. So why not put loving your family as your highest priority? That way, no matter what happens, you are guaranteed to have no regrets.

To find more time for your family, remove tasks from your schedule with a low ROTE — Return On Time and Energy, since you have a limited supply of time and energy. Eliminate, outsource, or delegate those activities with the lowest ROTE.

In this way, you can get more done at work and have more impact with your family in the same 24-hour day you had yesterday, with less worry, guilt, fear, and stress.

∽o∾

"The secret to comedy is . . . timing!" is an idea I learned from comedy writer Mike Price. This advice also applies to work-family prioritizing.

When your children are young, your family needs your time and attention. When your kids learn a new trick and yell to you, "Hey, look at me!" it matters that you're physically and emotionally available to watch and say, "Fantastic!"

I admit, I've told my little ones, "Do not have a tantrum right now. My schedule is really tight today. Maybe next Thursday I'll have time but for today, get a grip." I see now that I wasn't prioritizing.

When your children are grown and out on their own, if you want to increase the priority of your work, that's great. Maybe you go back to school or apply for a job with more responsibility or more travel. It all comes down to timing, giving your family members what they need when they need it.

In the Bible, it says, "There is a time for everything and a season for every activity under Heaven" (Ecc. 3:1). You can have it all, and do it all, just not all at once.

Accept Love, However It's Packaged

Fatherhood is pretending the present you love most is soap-on-a-rope.
Bill Cosby, American comedian

*Just because somebody doesn't love you the way you want them to,
doesn't mean they don't love you with all they have.*
Unknown

When I was pregnant with Mark, my neighbors offered to give me a baby shower. I wanted to be humble so I declined this honor. We all lost. They didn't get to celebrate the arrival of my first baby with me, and I missed the fun we could have had together.

In the same vein, when your family members want to love you, show up and let them. Over the years, my children have given me gaudy pins and stinky perfume as gifts. Before I learned this lesson of love, I often criticized their love-filled gifts and ended up hurting their feelings. I told myself I was giving them helpful feedback but really, I was rejecting their love.

Today, I wear their gifts and use them with pride. Homemade candles get burned, sparkly pins are worn, and artwork is displayed prominently.

⚭

One year for Christmas, we sent my mother-in-law some framed photos of her grandkids and a check for $1,000. I didn't have a shipping box for the gifts but since I had just bought a paper cutter, I put the gifts inside the paper cutter box. I wrapped the box in Christmas paper and then in brown shipping paper and mailed the package.

When she unwrapped the box, she assumed I had sent her a paper cutter as a gift. She didn't need a paper cutter, so she just took it down to her basement, unopened.

Almost a year later, I asked her about the package. When she finally admitted she never opened the box, I told her what was inside and she found her presents.

My question for you is: How often do you not open gifts of love because they weren't packaged the way you expected them? So open all packages of love. You never know what you'll find inside!

SUMMARY

Think about the legacy you want to leave and start to live those values now. Let your family be your first priority every day, with your work a close second. Prioritize tasks with the highest ROTE — Return On Time and Energy — and do those tasks first. Accept love, however it's packaged.

Action Items

1 Identify the changes you need to make in your life to leave the legacy you want.

2 Review your calendar for tasks with a high ROTE. Delegate, outsource or eliminate those with a low ROTE.

3 Show your love for your family!

PART 2

5 Key Lessons for Every Working Parent

A hug is worth a thousand words.

—Unknown

CHAPTER 5

One father is more than a hundred schoolmasters.
— George Herbert (1593–1633), Welsh poet and priest

An ounce of mother is worth a ton of priests.
— Spanish proverb

KEY LESSON #1:
Hug Your Kids Today

Baseball player Harmon Killebrew's father was playing with Harmon and his brother in the yard. His mother came out and said, "You're tearing up the grass."

"We're not raising grass," his dad replied. "We're raising boys."

∽o∾

Sure it's important to provide your children with food, clothing, and shelter ("and cell phone minutes," Amy adds). However, just as babies need to be held and touched to thrive, your children need to be hugged and loved to grow.

Children are social creatures — and so are you. We all need connections, both physical and emotional, with those we love. Hugs can break down barriers of conflict and build up bonds of love.

Hugs are simple but powerful expressions of our love, trust, belief, encouragement, and hope. That's a lot of reward for a hug!

Your kids need hugs throughout the day. In the morning, when they're anxious about a new kid in class, a social studies project or a spelling test, they need a hug. After a long, tough day, when words are not enough to revive or console your kids, they need another hug or two. And of course, bedtime wouldn't be complete without a hug.

It's always a good time, and the right time, for a hug.

ᏛᲿᏮ

When Alan Letzt, a former sales consulting client of mine, heard about the *Hug Your Kids Today* billboard project, he wrote:

The *Hug Your Kids Today* project is making a life-altering suggestion about the lasting importance of hugs. When our daughter Sabrina was alive, our family established and kept to our goal of 3 hugs per day — which resulted in more than 1,000 hugs per year for her 17 years. These hugs helped us enjoy the good times and work through the difficult times. Although Sabrina is no longer with us, we continue to feel the hugs and encouragement from her spirit, and strive to make her proud of us.

Hugging 101

A hug is like a boomerang — you get it back right away.
Bil Keane, Family Circus cartoonist

Hugs can do great amounts of good — especially for children.
Diana, Princess Of Wales (1961–1997)

ugging your children is not an original idea. I bet even cavemoms and cavedads hugged their kids thousands of years ago. That doesn't make hugging any less powerful today.

When you give a hug, don't settle for a quick squeeze-and-run. Below are the basic steps.

How to Give a Quality Hug

1. **Free your hands and arms.** Put down whatever is in your hands and arms. You need them to be empty to give a good hug.
2. **Empty your mind of distractions.** Clear your thoughts about work, your bills, the time, and other distractions.
3. **Make eye contact.** Get your loved one to your eye level, whether that means you sweep them up in your arms or you stand on a chair or stair.
4. **Then make heart contact.** Look them in the eye and tell them with great enthusiasm, "I love you. You matter to me. You mean the world to me," and everything else in your heart that you feel for them.
5. **Squeeze!** Then give them a genuine hug, squeeze them tightly, and whisper a love secret in their ear.

Don't multi-task when you hug. Hugs don't count if you're watching a sports game or the cooking channel on TV over the shoulder of a loved one when you're hugging them.

When you hug your kids, hug them as if it could be the last hug you'll ever give them. Hug them so thoroughly that when you part, you both walk away say, "Wow, now *that* was a hug!"

Let Your Family Know and Love the Real You

A father carries pictures where his money used to be.
Unknown

My mother had a great deal of trouble with me, but I think she enjoyed it.
Mark Twain (1835–1910), American humorist

The moment a child is born, the mother is also born. She never existed before. The woman existed, but the mother, never. A mother is something absolutely new.
Rajneesh, Indian mystic

I t's a risk to let your family know the real you because, like Achilles, it exposes your weak points. Take the risk and let your family know the real you so they can love the real you. Then get to know the real them. Your reward might be something like mine from years ago: A crude drawing of me that says, "Dear Mom, you are soo beautyful! Love, Amy."

∽o∾

Be outrageous. Share your crazy, wacky side with your family. For example, a few years ago, I took my kids to a monster truck rally. Once inside, I bought each of us a pirate flag to wave. We learned later that it was the symbol of the meanest, baddest monster truck, *The Gravedigger.* The whole event was very loud and dusty — and we laughed our heads off the entire time.

∽o∾

Ron traveled frequently in the 1980s and '90s. When Amy was about seven years old, she secretly tied this note to the neck of a life-sized, plastic rat and hid it in his suitcase:

Dear Dad,

This is a travel rat. Put him in your bed and sleep with him at night!

Love, Amy

Imagine his surprise when he opened his suitcase! Or the look on the faces of the TSA security screeners when they saw his travel rat go through their x-ray machines. For the next few years, Ron took his travel rat with him on all of his trips, until 2001 when the TSA tightened security. It is a cherished memento of her love for him.

∽o∽

For a short while, I spoke to groups as "Adventure Woman." I wore a red cape over my business suit and encouraged women to go on adventures. One night, just as I was leaving to give this speech, Amy, who was 12 years old at the time, slipped me this note:

Mom,

I just want you to know how proud I am of you. You are an utterly amazing person and I feel truly fortunate to be your daughter.

Love always, Amy, AKA Adventure Chick

Sometimes on Saturday mornings, Ron and Amy go for rides on his big motorcycle. Their first stop is for breakfast, and then they head out together, riding down some picturesque country roads. When they return, they're refreshed and have deepened a bond that sustains them through the challenges of the coming weeks.

∽o∽

Help your children value you for more than your paycheck. In a way, our children are like our customers or co-workers. We're partly responsible for how they perceive us. If we act like an ATM on two legs, how can we blame them for treating us that way? This is why sharing your time, ideas, values, and stories with your children matters. Let them see — and love — the real you.

◦◦◦

Keep your word with your family. I bet if you tell your co-worker or your clients that you'll have their project done by noon on Friday, you do whatever it takes to keep your word to them.

For the same reason, if you tell your family you're all going to the movies on Friday at 7:00 p.m., make sure you keep your word to them, too. Don't tell yourself, "Yes, but my in-box isn't empty." Do the tasks with the highest ROTE, then stop what you're doing and get thyself to the movies. The same goes with promises for vacations to Disneyland or scout campouts. If you say you'll go, go.

Your Teenagers Need Your Hugs Too

There's nothing wrong with teenagers that reasoning with them won't aggravate.
Unknown

Small boys become big men through the influence of big men who care about small boys.
Unknown

You can fool some of the people all of the time. And you can fool all of the people some of the time. But you can't fool Mom.
Unknown

Parenthood, it's not a job. It's an adventure!
Unknown

Many parents think that once their children are school-aged, their schedules and worries will get easier. That's usually true — for a while. However, once your children reach junior high, parenting gets

Teenagers need hugs too. (And sometimes, a haircut). Amy (center) with two teen friends.

more challenging because the stakes are higher. They can now get themselves into more serious trouble, like drugs, alcohol, gangs, or sex.

By high school, your teens have more homework, and their grades matter more, in terms of college applications or scholarships. On top of all this, teens are learning basic life skills, like how to manage their time and money — and drive a car! The stakes are high; they can't safely navigate these difficult times without you by their side.

∞⊙∽

At the same time that teenagers need your wisdom and experience, their hormones make them tougher to hug and love than their younger siblings. Teens can be prickly, distant, euphoric, argumentative, and downright unpleasant, and sometimes they cover all these moods in less than five minutes. The answer? It starts with a hug.

Mark's Proof of Love at the Bottom of His Backpack

They do not love that do not show their love.
William Shakespeare (1564–1616), English poet and playwright

During my piano recital, I was on a stage and scared. I looked at all the people watching me and saw my daddy waving and smiling. He was the only one doing that. I wasn't scared anymore.
A child

There are three stages of a man's life: He believes in Santa Claus, he doesn't believe in Santa Claus, he is Santa Claus.
Unknown

No matter how close you are to your children, they have secret lives when they are out of your sight, like at school, scouts, a friend's house, or even just playing alone in your backyard.

After Mark died, I was a little apprehensive to look in his hiding spots. I'm glad I did. I found the expected candy wrappers, small toys and shiny rocks, but it is the notes at the bottom of his school backpack that tell his story best.

There was a greeting card from his dad from the first day of school that year, on which Ron had written "Sometimes it's a little scary going to a new class. I used to be nervous too! Just remember to be yourself. You are one great son, Mark, and it won't take long for the kids in your class to find out what a great guy you are. Have fun and do well. Love, DAD."

There was another little card, which read, "You mean so much to me! Let us love one another for love comes from God. 1 John 4:7. Love, Mom."

Since Mark died during the summer, he'd carried these notes in his backpack every day that previous school year. They were touchstones that his dad and his mom really loved him. In addition to our hugs and words of love, Mark carried physical proof.

You don't have to wait for back-to-school time to give your family members proof of your love. Put notes in their lunches or text message them. Tell them how special they are to you and perhaps give them a word of encouragement; when you do, both of you feel better.

Hug Now! Don't Over-Think and Under-Hug

The road to Hell is paved with good intentions.
Unknown. From 16th century.

Dads don't need to be tall and broad-shouldered and clever. Love makes them so.
Pam Brown, Australian poet

Over-thinking can mess things up. It's easy to fall into the trap of telling yourself that now is not the best time to hug your kids or that you'll have more energy later. Hogwash. Right now is a perfect time to get out of your chair and give your children a hug. Don't over-think and under-do. Just hug them. Now.

Mark was a fussy baby but he would calm down if I put him in our wind-up baby swing. I once called the nurse at the doctor's office and asked, "Can you over-swing a baby?" She laughed but I pressed her, "No, really. He's been in the swing for three hours but he's sleeping."

Within the laws of common sense, you really can't over-swing a baby — and you really can't over-hug your children.

Maybe you worry you'll spoil your children. It's unlikely.

Maybe you worry you'll make them weak. As your children mature, they'll let you know how much hugging is enough for them.

Stop thinking. Start hugging. Now.

Hug Your Spouse

A hundred hearts would be too few, to carry all my love for you.
Unknown

Love is the irresistible desire to be irresistibly desired.
Mark Twain (1835–1910), American humorist

If love is blind, why is lingerie so popular?
Unknown

The most important thing a father can do for his children is to love their mother.
Theodore Hesburgh, president of University of Notre Dame

L et's face it — childhood is a time of constant change. Your children are continuously getting bigger, smarter, more capable, and more responsible. Sometimes other children join them in their family.

Still married after all these years. Ron and Michelle at beautiful Lake Tahoe in Nevada.

To deal with all this change, your children crave stability. The best form of stability for kids is having the same mother and father living together under the same roof their entire growing-up years. Although this isn't always possible, if your spouse is basically a good person, it's a worthy goal.

So besides hugging your kids, remember to hug your spouse every day too. It matters to your kids, your spouse, and you!

Note: When I write "spouse," that includes all spousal equivalents. For the purposes of brevity, I'll use "spouse" but if that's not your exact situation, translate it to suit your purposes.

Compete or Cooperate?

Like your job, love your wife.
Del, played by John Candy, from the movie *Planes, Trains and Automobiles*

Life's a bitch. Don't be one too.
Unknown

Love is a game that two can play and both win.
Eva Gabor (1919–1995), actress (married five times)

Competition between spouses can be a relationship killer, regardless of whether you're competing over money, titles, or perks. Focus your competitive drive at the office, with your co-workers, customers, and competitors. When you get home, turn it off and instead, use your *cooperative* drive with your family and loved ones.

∽∘∾

One way to cooperate is to avoid micromanaging your spouse. For example, Ron has always done the grocery shopping for our family, even when he was a vice-president of a big corporation. When other wives hear this, they usually ask me, "But what if he buys the wrong thing?"

"We eat it," I tell them. I might mention to him later that we prefer the fat-free version or the barbecue flavor but basically, we hush up. This sets a good example for our children, too, about flexibility and cooperation.

⌀⌀⌀

Try not to criticize how your spouse hugs or loves your kids. As long as the children are safe, let your spouse love them his or her own way. My research turned up complaints from men that women would sometimes walk right up and criticize a man's parenting skills in ways that would be considered rude if she said the same thing to another woman.

The Lesson of Three Things

A wife lasts only for the length of the marriage, but an ex-wife is there for the rest of your life.
Jim Samuels, American comedian

Infatuation is when you think he's as sexy as Robert Redford, as smart as Henry Kissinger, as noble as Ralph Nader, as funny as Woody Allen, and as athletic as Jimmy Connors.
Love is when you realize that he's as sexy as Woody Allen, as smart as Jimmy Connors, as funny as Ralph Nader, as athletic as Henry Kissinger and nothing like Robert Redford — but you'll take him anyway.
Judith Viorst, author, *Redbook* magazine, 1975

The best relationship advice I ever got was from a sales trainer. I was in an all-day workshop on how to sell more, but the idea that has stayed with me 25 years was the "Lesson of Three Things." I apologize that I don't recall the speaker's name.

The trainer was recently re-married and he was reflecting that when he was married to his first wife, he eventually found she did three things that really bugged him.

So he divorced her and married another woman who didn't do those three things — but he soon discovered that she did three other things that got on his nerves.

The lesson, of course, is that it is inevitable that your spouse is going to have a few aspects that irritate you, but if he or she is a moral, loving person, these irritating habits don't have to crater your marriage or relationship.

&oo&

If divorce is inevitable, the best contract clause I ever heard of was from a couple I'll call Tom and Sandy. They didn't want to criticize each other in front of the children so they agreed to pay $100 per word of any sentence that was critical of the ex-spouse. So if Tom said to his kids, "Your mother is so lazy," he'd have to pay Sandy $500. No criticism was worth that kind of penalty — and after several years, neither party had had to pay up. Who won? Everybody — Tom, Sandy, and their kids.

SUMMARY

Children need to be hugged, touched and loved to develop, even when they're teenagers. Let your family get to know the real you. Keep your word to your family. It's important to hug your spouse and cooperate, not compete, with him or her.

Action Items
❶ Accept that your children never outgrow the need to be hugged.
❷ Hug your kids — and your spouse — right now!

HUGS FROM MICHELLE'S FRIENDS

ere are some "hugs" from my friends. They represent men and women who are experts in Internet advertising, physical therapy, computers, perseverance, and law — from Nevada to Michigan. Enjoy!

Dick Larkin, Illinois
Internet advertising entrepreneur and father of a school-aged daughter

I recently delivered a presentation for which I received so much praise that, by the end of the day, I could barely get my head through my hotel room door. My power trip did not last long.

In the pre-dawn hours, my cell phone rang and in a flat and measured voice, my wife simply said, "There's been a fire." An improperly installed fireplace insert in our new home had ignited the insulation inside the wall. Our daughter had been sleeping so soundly in her second floor bedroom that she never heard the wailing smoke detectors. It was only with my wife's repeated shaking and urging that our daughter gained consciousness in time for the two of them to flee the smoke-filled house.

In an instant, my priorities were upended. This one call helped me remember what is truly meaningful instead of just material. I no longer let a day go by without giving both of them an extra hug.

Sherise Smith, Nevada
Physical therapist and mother of three school-aged boys

I was Michelle's next-door neighbor on that life-changing day in July 1998. Just a few days earlier, Michelle had sat on my couch discussing Mark's strange flu and what to do about it. Then overnight, our lives were turned upside down.

The thing that impressed me the most about Michelle after Mark's death was her incredible faith. I realized the strength of her faith and started to explore my own faith.

When my life became overly scheduled as a "part-time" hospital administrator, it did not take me long to leap to the decision to work less and mommy more. It made me realize that it is indeed quantity, as well as quality, that counts.

To me, hugging my kids every day encompasses many things. For my now-teenage son who once idolized Mark as the older boy next door, hugging means buying him his favorite sandwich and delivering it to the front seat of his truck at school as a surprise. It means taking the time to learn how to text message with my kids. For all my boys, it means taking the time to listen to them every single day.

Carol Steffanni, Michigan

An information technology director for the state of Michigan, mother of two grown daughters, and grandmother of four beautiful grandchildren – soon to be five!

When my daughters were school-aged, as soon as they came home from school, they would call me at work. No matter what I was doing, I would answer their calls and listen to their joys or woes (or both!) of the day. To this day, they still call me to talk over their problems or share exciting news. Throughout their lives, we've stayed connected via the phone.

I also included them in my work when possible. I've been in politics all my career and both of my girls have "worked the campaign trail." They have walked in parades, sealed envelopes, cheered at rallies, and attended inaugural parties. My oldest daughter, now in her 30's, actually called one day and thanked me for "dragging her to all those events" because she now had the social skills to mingle and carry on discussions with people she didn't know.

We also established special rituals. For example, for back-to-school shopping, we picked a day to get up early, shop, have lunch, and shop some more. Once a year, all the adult women in my extended family gather for Women's Weekend. We meet at someone's house and we Christmas shop all weekend. I'm the oldest of eight children, and most of us have children, so it's a large gathering. We start Friday night and go until Sunday with food, drinks, shopping, laughing, sometimes crying, and bonding . . . aunts, sisters, nieces, sisters-in-law, and Grandma. This ritual strengthens our bonds of love, which carry through the generations.

Ruben Gonzalez, Texas

Three-time Olympian, professional speaker and author on perseverance, and father of two home-schooled children

I show my family every day how much I love them by spending a lot of time with them. I fix them breakfast, and whenever I take a break from work, I play with them. I read them bedtime stories, too.

Home schooling gives us the flexibility to travel whenever we want so we take lots of short family vacations. I regularly take my kids on errands with me and I've even flown my seven year old daughter with me when I speak across America. Spending time with my kids is a great way to show them I love them but the best way is by loving their mom — my wife, Cheryl.

Bonnie Drinkwater, Nevada

Attorney in private practice and mother of two young children

One of the ways I show my love to my family is we eat dinner together. It isn't easy with my husband's and my evening commitments and my kids' extracurricular activities, but we have made it a priority.

Over our dinner, we can connect as a family, find out what has happened in everyone's day, and make plans for the next day (or month or year.) We don't allow any television or phone calls. We laugh a lot and truly enjoy each other's company. This time together is sacred and cherished.

CHAPTER 6

Before becoming a mother, I had a hundred theories on how to bring up children. Now I have seven children and only one theory: Love them, especially when they least deserve to be loved.
—Kate Samperi, advice columnist for *Women's Day* magazine

Considering how expensive it is, experience ought to be the best teacher.
—Unknown

KEY LESSON #2:
Carpe Kids

Robin Williams, as Mr. Keating in the movie *Dead Poets Society,* encouraged his students to *carpe diem* (Latin for *seize the day.*) I suggest you *carpe kids,* which I translate to *seize what's positive about your kids.* Another way to say this idea is, "Don't *carpe crap,*" that is, don't look for the negative.

Face it, your kids are going to do stupid things, forget stuff, and make mistakes. Heck, you do, too and you have a lot more experience and maturity under your belt. When it happens to your child, the trick is to focus on what they did right. I admit this lesson is the hardest of the five for me to use consistently.

It's Not You, It's Me

This key lesson dawned upon me at a time when Ron, Amy, and our new son Devin were each going to the psychologist every week. Initially I felt smug, thinking I was the only one in the family without problems. Then I suddenly realized — perhaps I *was* the problem!

After I visited the therapist a few times, (then we were *all* seeing her!) I became aware that I held perfection as my standard for myself and my family members. Since by definition, humans are not perfect, in my eyes we were all constantly falling below the standard. As a result, I was very critical because I was trying to get us all to be perfect.

If you compare your kids to your idea of perfection like I did, stop. Instead, compare them to happy people. Learn to appreciate them just the way they are right now, not how they could be, if only they would pick up their room or finish their report on Antarctica that's due tomorrow.

వింం

No matter how sincere your intentions are to be a super working parent, crazy stuff happens. You might put out the book report that you and your child sweated over all night, so your spouse can see it, and you accidentally leave it at home. Maybe over breakfast your little one announces she needs a princess costume and two dozen cookies — that day. One morning recently, Devin told me he needed to have the first 30 U.S. presidents memorized by the next day, and he didn't even know the first 10.

And just when you think things couldn't get any more chaotic, they usually do. There are times when you aren't sure you're even going to *survive* parenthood. That's why seeing the positive side of any situation is so powerful. It helps you respond more lovingly during challenging times.

Forget Perfection; Look for the Positive

No statue has even been put up to a critic.

Jean Sibelius (1865–1957), Finnish composer

It is not the critic who counts; not the man who points out how the strong man stumbles or where the doer of deeds could have done better. The credit belongs to the man who is actually in the arena, whose face is marred by dust and sweat and blood, who strives valiantly, who errs and comes up short again and again, because there is no effort without error or shortcoming, but who knows the great enthusiasms, the great devotions, who spends himself for a worthy cause; who, at the best, knows, in the end, the triumph of high achievement, and who, at the worst, if he fails, at least he fails while daring greatly, so that his place shall never be with those cold and timid souls who knew neither victory nor defeat.

President Theodore Roosevelt (1858–1919)

When Amy was ten years old, she qualified for the Scripps spelling bee held at her school. There was a teacher stationed near the spellers, whose job was to comfort the kids when they misspelled a word and were therefore out of the bee.

Amy held on for five rounds until she spelled "delicious" as "delicous." What were the first words from the comforting teacher? "You forgot the second 'i'!"

What happened to "Good try. I'm so proud of you" or "Good luck next year"? Yet how often have we had similar critical reactions to our own children's mistakes?

∽o∾

I read an article about a young woman who earned perfect scores on both her SAT and ACT exams. I wanted to say to Amy, "See? Perfection is attainable. If she can reach perfection, why can't you?"

Then I read this young woman's advice for future students taking the test. She told them not to stress about the tests because there are many other things that matter more than test scores. This high school senior was far ahead of my game — her test scores were perfect and yet she was telling others how they weren't all that important in the bigger picture.

Coach or Critic?

While dealing with a stranger, common courtesy you use,
But the family you love, you seem to abuse.
Unknown

The beatings will continue until morale improves.
Unknown

Affirming words from moms and dads are like light switches. Speak a word of affirmation at the right moment in a child's life and it's like lighting up a whole roomful of possibilities.
Gary Smalley, American author

Have you ever noticed that sometimes you treat your co-workers, and even strangers, with more kindness and gentleness than you do members of your own family?

I used to tell myself that I wasn't "critical," rather, I "gave my children a lot of feedback, both good and bad." In reality, I had a critical tongue and then I balanced my sharp words with a large heaping of praise. Which words do you think my children remembered? My criticisms, I'm afraid.

Jeanette Clift George, the founder of the theater group The A.D. Players in Houston, once said that when you ring a bell, you hear it three times: when you ring it, when it echoes, and when you remember the sound later. Criticism, especially from a parent, is like ringing a bell. It reverberates in a child's mind long after it's over.

∽o∾

Rather than being a critic, try being your child's coach. Good coaches are always looking for what their students are doing right, and encouraging them when they are weak. You can be your child's greatest coach because you know their strengths the best.

I recall author Dr. Wayne Dyer many years ago suggesting that if your child gets 5 questions wrong out of 20 on a test, ignore the 5 he missed and focus on the 15 he got right. If he didn't get any right, focus on how well he spelled his name at the top of the page. If he didn't spell his name right, at least congratulate him for finding his classroom.

∽o∾

To be a good coach, you don't have to be original. I once taped a copy of Maryanne Williamson's famous poem, which Nelson Mandela used in his 1994 inaugural speech, to Amy's bathroom mirror. It begins, "Our deepest fear is not that we are inadequate. Our deepest fear is that we are powerful beyond measure. It is our light, not our darkness, that frightens us most."

To which I added:

Amy — You are powerful beyond measure! Love, Mom

P.S. Eat a good breakfast, empty the dishwasher, pack a lunch, and feed the dogs. I love you!

∽o∾

On a rare occasion, you may be a coach unintentionally. Mark Katz, Bill Clinton's joke writer, said in his book, *Clinton & Me,* that when he introduced the President to his parents, Clinton launched into a tribute of Mark's comic gifts. His mother replied, "You just complimented Mark for the same things I used to spank him for."

Seeing Your Child's Glass Half-Full

It is not until you become a mother that your judgment slowly turns to compassion and understanding.

Erma Bombeck (1927–1996), American humorist

To belittle is to be little.

Unknown

One of the advantages of being a parent is you know your children well enough to discover their tender spots and you are also close enough to zing them there. For example, Devin is small for his age, so he is sensitive about being called a "baby."

Calling him a "baby" was a verbal club I used to grab when he made a mistake. Then I realized that few of us improve by being belittled or insulted. Now I try to act like his coach and unemotionally help him clean up his mess or fix his mistake, learn how to prevent it, and move on.

When you stop expecting perfection of your children and instead look for what's positive, then you're happier and your kids are happier too. It's a way to teach them to look for what's "in the glass," even on those occasions when it's only one-eighth full.

໙໐໙

One good way to help you look for what's positive is to imagine a picture frame around a not-so-good situation. Around this picture frame, it says "What's good about this situation?" So the next time you see that your child has left the bathroom a mess, by asking yourself what's good, perhaps you can appreciate that they care about their cleanliness or looking sharp. Or maybe if they left their good coat on the school bus during a cold spell in January, the positive aspect is they will get a chance to develop their compassion for those less fortunate who don't own a warm coat.

Sure, they still have to straighten up the bathroom or wear an alternate coat for a day, but by seeing what's positive, you win two ways. First, you save yourself the energy of losing your temper over typical kid behavior and spare yourself the guilt that follows. Second, in the long run, you teach your child to look for the positive in situations and thereby pass on this important lesson to the next generation.

〰️

To teach yourself to see what's positive in any situation, you might want to keep a gratitude journal. I actually got this idea from Bonnie, one of the gals in my book club. Every day, I challenge myself to list three things I'm grateful for — and usually it's four or five. You'll be amazed how quickly you begin to notice things that happen during your day that make you think, "I'll have to remember to write that down in my gratitude journal tomorrow."

Love Your Kids for Who They Are, Not What They Are

THANK YOU FREAKS
Banner in a scene in the Disney movie, *Madagascar*

I wish they would only take me as I am.
Vincent Van Gogh (1853–1890), Dutch artist

t's easy to be your children's biggest fan when they're hitting the ball or shooting baskets consistently or getting As on their spelling tests week after week. Real love is being their number one fan when they haven't made it to first base or been able to swim one length of the pool all season, or when they can barely spell "cat."

Kids need to feel valuable for who they are, not what they've accomplished. Remind your kids on a daily basis that they are valuable simply because they are yours. Your children are important to you and your family no matter what the rest of the world says. Their accomplishments are just the sprinkles on the cake.

This holds true even if your children are top performers. They need to know that you think it's great that they just won the ski race or first place in the science fair but it really isn't related to how you value them.

Mark's standardized academic tests showed he was in the top 1% of all students nationwide, yet we don't focus on remembering his intelligence; we concentrate on his kindness. One of his fellow gifted students, when asked what she remembered about him, said that on Popsicle days, he always saved her her favorite flavor. Mark's last teacher, Jackie Swobe Borsum, commented:

Mark was recognized for his ability to learn things quickly and his exceptional intelligence but what really impressed me about Mark was his kind heart. He was always willing to help another child with their work or to assist in any way. If someone was hurt during P.E., Mark offered to help them up. Following lessons, he would thank me for working hard and doing a good job — this is not normal student behavior.

Hugs — Mark gave such big, warm hugs. His big smile warmed my heart. He taught me to never take for granted a hug from a child. His hugs were so consuming that he often nearly knocked me down. So many sweet hugs that I will always cherish.

A student teacher in his class, Geary Scully, wrote:

Mark was incredibly gifted; his greatest gift was the love he gave, not only to his family but to those around him. On several occasions as I looked over the heads of students, trying to gain some control at lunchtime, Mark would sneak up and give me the biggest bear hug, squeezing the breath out of me. He wouldn't say anything, but he didn't have to.

∽o∾

When my children were little, after I'd tuck them into bed, I'd stand over them, give a big sigh and say, "Isn't (s)he wonderful?" The sigh released all my frustrations from the day — the accidents, unkind words, and disappointments. My hope was they'd fall asleep knowing I thought they were wonderful no matter how the day had gone, and I loved them. I hope you have your own positive bedtime rituals.

SUMMARY

When things go wrong for your children, look for what's positive. Act like your children's coach, not their critic. Don't measure them against your idea of perfection.

Action Items

❶ Look for what your kids are doing right, regardless of the circumstances.

❷ Show your love for each of your family members today.

HUGS FROM MICHELLE'S FRIENDS

hese "hugs" from my friends represent men and women who are experts in communications, leadership, entrepreneurship, sales, inventing, and serving at-risk children — from California to Ohio. Listen up!

Erin Meehan Breen, Nevada
Writer and single mother of three school-aged children

I know my teenage son didn't mean to fall in with the wrong crowd. He didn't mean to get mixed up in drugs and alcohol. And I knew getting him out would take a drastic move.

That summer in the Marine Military Academy got him back on track. And it opened his eyes to the fact that he didn't need to follow others; he could lead them.

For me, the best way to see the positive in my children has been to see beyond the situation at hand to each child's true potential.

He's now a 4.0 student headed to a career in physics.

Mark Sanborn, Colorado
Author and speaker on leadership, and father of two school-aged boys

Our family received a "You are special plate" as a gift and we use it with guests as well as family members. At mealtime, the special person who has the red plate gets to hear what everyone else at the table likes about them. We make sure that each of our boys regularly gets the plate, so that the family can tell him how special he is and why. This is a great way to focus on the positive and affirm our love.

Ruvi De Guzman, California

Entrepreneur and mother of three children

My firstborn was born with a medical condition and had to have his leg amputated below his knee at birth. The moment he was born, our eyes locked and I whispered in his ear, "God picked me to be your mommy, and we have a purpose and a journey together." As he grew up, it was a challenge to juggle his medical appointments with all my corporate travel and business meetings, but I kept my eye on how, by our example, we would help other families.

By keeping his and my focus on what he could do, not what he couldn't, he's grown up to be extremely social with a sweet soul and a great sense of humor. He skis, rides a bike, works out, skateboards, snowboards, and swims; he even wrestled on the high school wrestling team. He is now on his way to college. By our modeling a positive attitude, my other children have learned acceptance, compassion and patience.

What is "normal" anyway? We are all broken in our own way. "None of us is perfect," is what I tell all my children — and remind myself.

Hal Becker, Ohio

Sales consultant and dad of a teenage daughter

I learned from my daughter when she was young that when I grounded her (only twice), ten minutes later she would come out of her bedroom and ask, "Can we play now?"

Kids hold onto nothing! That is my biggest lesson — to never stay mad at friends and family, and when "stuff" happens, I just want to play later too.

Julie Savage, Texas

Award-winning inventor and mother of three adopted, school-aged boys

As the mother of three busy boys, I used to make the mistake of looking at my kids through a microscope. I inspected everything they did and compared them to other children, our unrealistic expectations, and the neighbor's "perfect family." This blew their faults out of proportion, because our view was too narrow and focused. It led to frustrated parents and broken-hearted kids.

I learned to throw away my microscope and instead, view them through a telescope. A telescope is a wonderful device because it makes faraway objects appear much closer. I also look at my kids through a lens of faith, believing that one day, we will see the results of the seeds that we are planting now. This approach helps me look past the things I may find today — such as a bad grade on a math test, a broken window, or dirty socks stuffed under the sofa — and see their positive aspects right now.

Kathleen Sandoval, Nevada

Program director for a non-profit agency serving at-risk youth, and mother of three school-aged children

Many of the youth our agency serves are raised in a negative world. They have been abused, neglected and pushed out of their homes or are on the run or live with parents who abuse drugs. As a result, these kids have no supervision and have to rely on themselves. It also makes it easy for them to become part of the cycle of abusing others, abusing drugs, failing school and getting involved in the juvenile correctional system. Our most important job at the agency is to stop this negative and destructive cycle.

If these kids just had a hug and someone to tell them something positive about themselves on a daily basis, maybe the cycle would never even get started.

After serving children all day who weren't loved, hugged, and told how wonderful they are, when I come home I can't wait to hug my kids and tell them how much I love them!

CHAPTER 7

(S)He who laughs, lasts.
⌐Mary Pettibone Poole, author

The most wasted of all days is one without laughter.
⌐e. e. cummings (1894–1962), American poet

If you can't make it better, laugh at it.
⌐Erma Bombeck (1927–1996), American humorist

KEY LESSON #3:
When All Else Fails, Laugh

Have you ever noticed how you're naturally attracted to people who can make you laugh? Maybe they tell funny jokes, do impressions or they just make funny observations. As Norman Cousins, the author of *Anatomy of Illness*, proved, laughter is powerful medicine, no matter whether it's taken like an antibiotic, to cure a problem, or like a vitamin, to keep trouble away.

My dad always told me that when things go wrong, I can laugh or I can cry. He's right — laughter can be a conscious choice even if you don't feel like laughing at the time. For example, I used to teach Sunday school and every week I'd ask the children for their prayer requests.

Usually they mentioned their sick grandmas or lost pets but I had one fourth grade boy who had the same prayer request every week for an entire year — better school lunches. I could have gotten annoyed. Instead, I chose to laugh.

∽o∾

In our family, I ask our children to make all our birthday and holiday cards, so I can hear what they really want to say.

When Devin was six years old, his card to me said:

Happy Birthday Mom, I wish you were donuts.

"Donuts?" I asked him. He explained that he loved me, but he loved donuts just a little bit more. Instead of feeling insulted, I laughed at his creativity and honesty.

When he was seven, he made me a Mother's Day card with a drawing of a beautiful green chameleon on the cover. On the inside, it said:

L is for the way you look at me
O is for the overrated hating
V is for very very extraordinary
E is for everything you've done.
I LOVE YOU.

I recognized the pattern because we had just bought the movie *The Parent Trap,* and he had adapted the theme song from it for my card.

"Overrated hating?" I asked. He said he had no idea what it meant. I laughed, gave him a hug, and told him how much I liked the card.

A few years later, he made me another card:

Happy Birthday

M — Mild

O — Omnivore

M — Mom

"Omnivore?" What about Outrageous, Optimistic or Organized?

What a hoot! Hallmark look out. When you are able to love your kids in the moment, even if they've done something that doesn't look particularly loving but you know that their intent was to love, everyone wins.

The Superpower of Humor

Laugh and the world laughs with you. Cry and you . . . have to blow your nose.
A first-grade student

Through humor, you can soften some of the worst blows that life delivers. And once you find laughter, no matter how painful your situation might be, you can survive it.
Bill Cosby, American comedian

Just as Superman can fly and Wonder Woman can lift a car, you can use your superpowers of humor and laughter with your kids to change how they feel about themselves, their situation and even you. Humor's power comes from the truth that we all make mistakes.

Humor is so powerful it can connect you to your child along paths that logical words and dutiful actions cannot travel. For example, when Mark was very young, he was afraid of a small mechanical cow. I could wind it up, put it in a doorway and he would not go out of that door as long as that cow was walking and mooing.

Now, whenever we see one of these cows in a store, we think of him. Maybe if he'd grown up and gone to college, I might have bought him another cow and sent it along with him to remind him not to be afraid — and that his mother loved him.

∽o∾

Treat laughter like your everyday silverware. Use it daily. Don't save it for special occasions, like you do your fancy china dishes.

When you use humor with your children, remember Spiderman's motto: With great power comes great responsibility. It's important that you use laughter to help and heal, not to hurt. Sarcasm is for mature audiences only; young kids don't understand it and saying "I was only kidding" later doesn't take away all the sting.

It's said that you only use 10% of your brain; you probably only use 10% of your funny bone too. Train yourself that when things go wrong to look for what's funny about the situation.

The Healing Power of Humor

Bad spellers of the world, untie!
Graffiti

Always laugh when you can. It is cheap medicine.
Lord Byron (1788–1824), English poet

Even if there is nothing to laugh about, laugh on credit.
Anonymous

umor comforts and softens the feelings of failure or falling short of our goals. It can also help you and your children reframe a bad situation, which can open your minds to other possible solutions. For example, let's say one of your kids overlooked a key factor and a project didn't turn out the way they'd planned. The following story might help you reduce your child's embarrassment.

Sherlock Holmes and Dr. Watson go on a camping trip. After a good dinner, they climb in their tent and go to sleep.

Some hours later, Holmes wakes up and nudges his faithful friend. "Watson, look up at the sky and tell me what you see."

"I see millions and millions of stars, Holmes" replies Watson.

"And what do you deduce from that?"

Watson ponders for a minute. "Well, astronomically, it tells me that there are millions of galaxies and potentially billions of planets. Astrologically, I observe that Saturn is in Leo. Horologically, I deduce that the time is approximately a quarter past three. Meteorologically, I suspect that we will have a beautiful day tomorrow. Theologically, I can see that God is all powerful, and that we are a small and insignificant part of the universe. "

But what does it tell you, Watson?"

Watson is silent for a moment.

"Watson, you idiot!" says Holmes. "Someone has stolen our tent!

At the end of a recent winter break, I told my children about a boy from Mexico named Diego whom I read about in the newspaper. He glued his hand to his headboard to avoid going back to school.

One Big, Happy, Funny Family

Have you ever belched just because you're bored?
One of my kids, who remains anonymous

Genetics or environment — either way, we're in trouble.
Amy Nichols

Families are like fudge ... mostly sweet with a few nuts.
Unknown

Art Linkletter and Bill Cosby co-hosted a show called "Kids Say the Darnedest Things." I've never met a parent — or grandparent — that didn't have a few funny stories to share about their young ones. I'm sure you have yours. Here are a few of mine:

We saw a license plate that said "EBAYMOM" and Devin, age 9, commented, "How sad. They had to buy their mom on eBay."

〰♦〰

When Amy was in third grade, she brought home a notice from school that asked parents to come and speak about their jobs at an upcoming Career Day.

"Would you like me to come and tell the boys and girls in your class about what it's like to be in sales?" I offered.

She replied, "Oh Mom. Why can't you be something interesting? Why can't you be a pharmacist?"

〰♦〰

I take my children with me to hear the political candidates when they come to town to speak. When one candidate had boxes of free donuts, Devin at age 10 said, "Free donuts? Wow! I am *so* voting for this guy!"

〰♦〰

I was driving Amy (then 14) on errands and we saw a license plate holder that said, "100% Dolphin Queen." I asked her if she thought the driver was a fan of the Miami Dolphin football team, or did she want to swim with the dolphins?

Amy replied, "Mom, dolphins are the only animals other than humans that have sex for fun. Maybe she's *that* kind of Dolphin Queen."

Laugh Sooner

Humor is truth — only faster.
Gilda Radner (1946–1989), American comedienne

Comedy is tragedy plus time.
Carol Burnett, American comedienne

There is a thin line that separates laughter and pain, comedy and tragedy, humor and hurt.
Erma Bombeck (1927–1996), American humorist

aughter is like voting in Chicago. You should laugh early and often. I recall reading about a woman who, after a catastrophe, reminded her co-workers they were going to laugh about this someday, why not start now? That's good advice when you're raising kids. If you spend enough time with children, something crazy is bound to happen. Why wait to laugh?

When Devin was 10, he had an 8:00 a.m. appointment with his therapist to discuss ways to control his impulsivity. At the end of his 50-minute session, we noticed a cylindrical lump in his sock. When we pulled it out, it was my nickel collection!

Apparently, he'd seen the collection in my bedroom that morning and on impulse, put it in his sock. What else could I do but laugh at the irony?

✎o✎

Devin was doing his homework at the dining room table recently where there was a flower arrangement that my parents had sent for my birthday. As he was working on a math worksheet, he turned to me and said, "Your flowers are dying, Mom, so I ate some." Ah, another opportunity for me to laugh.

Laugh at Yourself

If you can learn to laugh at yourself, you'll never run out of things to laugh about.

Unknown

If you can't laugh at yourself, you may be missing the colossal joke of the century.

Dame Edna, character played by Australian Barry Humphries

My friend Deb had all the classic symptoms of a heart attack, so she called a neighbor who whisked her off to the local emergency room.

After the technicians cut off her favorite camisole, she began to feel a bit better. Then someone asked her if she'd like something to eat, and one turkey sandwich later, she felt good enough to be released to go home.

Most people would be too embarrassed to admit it cost them hundreds of dollars in medical bills to fix a too-tight camisole and low blood sugar, but not Deb. She paid the damages and had a good laugh at herself.

∽o∾

I have an Old English sheepdog named Oreo who has a bad habit of stealing food off the kitchen counters. One day, he stole and ate an entire cube of butter. I was so mad at him that I gave him a long speech about how much more expensive butter was than margarine.

He just sat there, licked his lips, and looked at me. Then I realized how silly I sounded and laughed my head off.

I took my kids to a monster truck rally. After I got them seated, I saw there was a Starbucks coffee cart, so I headed over. I asked the coffee cart lady, "Is the decaf fresh?"

She said, "Honey, we don't sell decaf at a monster truck rally." Ha!

Devin gets busted! Notice the sign near his stomach says, "DO NOT CLIMB."

SUMMARY

When things go wrong for your children, look for ways you can laugh with them about it. Humor is powerful; it can connect you to your family and even heal pain, so use it every day. Learn to laugh at yourself, too.

Action Items

1 Practice looking for what's funny in all situations. This will help you develop the skill of seeing what's funny when you or your kids make mistakes.

2 Watch some funny movies with your family so you can laugh together.

HUGS FROM MICHELLE'S FRIENDS

hese "hugs" are from men and women who are experts in branding, public schools, sales, business, marketing, and time management — from Nevada to New Jersey. Enjoy!

Joe Calloway, Tennessee

Business author and speaker on branding, restaurant owner, and father of two daughters

My daughters are preschool-aged — and I'm in my 50s! My wife and I had our first daughter the old-fashioned way then adopted our youngest girl from China. To me, a key to this whole child-raising business is a matter of perspective. I remember when we let our first daughter try using a spoon for the first time. Within what seemed like a nanosecond, she had splattered the entire kitchen with baby food. The walls were covered, the ceiling was covered, and we were covered! My wife and I looked at each other and just broke out in laughter. It was a mess . . . a joyful, glorious, wonderful mess. We always try to remember the blessing of the messes that come with these two little girls!

Rebecca Fox, Texas

Elected trustee for a large school district and mother of two teenagers

While I am a huge believer in using laughter instead of anger with my kids, I learned that my kids can use this lesson back on me too. One day when my son was in high school, he said, "Mom, remember how you always say that someday we're going to look back on this moment and laugh? Well, keep that in mind. Here's my report card." His cleverness totally disarmed me and I had to laugh.

When my daughter was in junior high, she borrowed a dress from me. The next time I put it on I was shocked to see the length had been considerably shortened. When I complained that she'd altered it without asking me, she said, "But you said I could borrow it!" One glimpse in the mirror turned my anger and shock into laughter.

Dan Seidman, Illinois

Sales speaker, trainer, and father of three school-aged children, including twin girls

When our daughter lost her first tooth, she was so excited. At bedtime, she knew that the tooth fairy was going to lay some money on her. When my wife and I went to bed, being spectacular parents, we forgot about her tooth. The next morning, our crying daughter awakened us. "The tooth fairy forgot me," she wailed.

I mumbled something about the 2006 census revealing an influx of six year olds who are losing their teeth in the spring. "Honey, we're positive the tooth fairy will be here tonight," I assured her.

Later that day my wife and I bumped into Laurie, a friend with kids the same age. She told us, "I've got you beat. When our son lost his first tooth, we forgot to put money under the pillow. He came into our room bawling and I told him to go to the bathroom and clean up while I checked myself. As he sniffled his way in to wash up, I dove into my purse — and could only find a twenty-dollar bill! Oh well, it went right under his pillow. He was deliriously happy — but all the parents at his school now hate my guts."

Jane Sandlar, New Jersey

Serial entrepreneur and mother of two teenage boys

Teenagers offer so many opportunities to laugh. Like when my oldest son wanted to have dreadlocks for his senior picture. He was not into the drug culture — he just liked the look. While I loved his long curly locks, being the liberal mother that I am, I gave in. He went to an area where they knew how to do dreads, and got them done. They turned out horrible. We learned the hard way that Caucasian dreads are not done the same way as African-American dreads. We tried shampoos, detergent, dishwashing liquid, Oxyclean — and ultimately mineral oil, to get them out. Then, with the help of an Internet kit, a patient mom, and 17 hours later (a real mother-son bonding experience) we had our Jewish Rastafarian son!

David Avrin, Colorado

Marketing and branding speaker, and father of three school-aged children

I like to show my family that you can be silly and irreverent at any age. I recently stopped at the grocery store with my daughter. Once inside the door, I made a beeline toward the produce section, grabbed a Chiquita banana sticker off the bunch, and promptly stuck it smack in the middle of my forehead. "Oh my gosh Daddy, please don't do that!" my young daughter implored me. Of course, I ignored her request.

As I walked around the store, acting as if there was nothing out of the ordinary, my daughter did everything she could to pretend that she wasn't with me. Her horror only encouraged me. "You are so embarrassing, Dad," she said to me.

"Are you kidding?" I replied. "I haven't even begun to embarrass you! Just ask your older sister." She just rolled her eyes.

From others in the store, I got a few surprised and confused looks, but mostly smiles. Perhaps many of them were hearkening back to their childhoods when they wouldn't be caught dead in a supermarket without a Chiquita banana sticker on their forehead. Or was that just me?

Tammy Ingraham, Nevada

Speaker and writer on time management, and mother of five children

One afternoon, my children came home from school, and as they were filing in the door, I was assigning chores to each one. By the time I got to my last little guy, he disgustedly looked up at me and retorted, "Gosh Mom, I came home from school to be with you, not to be worked to death!" At first, I was tempted to launch into my whole "we work as a family to keep our home nice for our family" speech, and then as I looked at his little freckled cheeks, flushed with anger, I scooped him up in my arms and we tumbled to the floor in laughter!

That day I was reminded how important it is to greet my children at the door, hug each one as they come in, and let them know that seeing them is the best part of my day!

CHAPTER 8

Patience with others is Love. Patience with self is Hope. Patience with God is Faith.

— Adel Bestavros (1924–2005), Egyptian lawyer and preacher

We are all of us, from birth to death, guests at a table which we did not spread. The sun, the earth, love, friends, our very breath are parts of the banquet ... Shall we think of the day as a chance to come nearer to our Host, and to find out something of Him who has fed us so long?

— Rebecca Harding Davis (1831–1910), American author

On a long journey of human life, faith is the best of companions; it is the best refreshment on the journey; and it is the greatest property.

— Buddha, circa 500 BC, founder of Buddhism

KEY LESSON #4:
Develop Your Family's Faith Life

If you've ever been though a tough time, you know that no one gets through it alone. Most people rely on one or more of the following: professional therapy; family or close friends; drugs or alcohol; distractions like TV, eating or shopping; or their faith in God. Only the last one — God and my faith — worked for me. This is almost ironic, since God is the most powerful force in the universe.

To me, life is like a basketball game. Regardless of my circumstances, if I had to put together my Dream Team, my first pick would be God. Anyone who's powerful enough to part the Red Sea, I want on my team.

∽ o ∾

If you don't believe in God, that's your choice. 83% of Americans do, and 86% have some faith affiliation. That's according to a study of 35,000 Americans over age 18, released by the Pew Forum on Religion and Public Life in February 2008.

You might wonder how I can believe in a God that allows innocent little children to die. I can because He's the same God that made Mark, gave him to me, let me be his mother his whole life and when he was taken from my arms, God comforted me and sent people to hug me, teach me, and walk with me through my grief.

I admit, before Mark died, I was not particularly active in my faith. Our family went to church regularly but I pretty much forgot about God the rest of the week. After Mark died, I felt God slide up next to me and walk alongside me. I never felt alone, not for one moment. He held my hand, whispered soothing words in my ears, and steadied me.

Developing our family's faith. Amy, Michelle and Ron (L to R).

You might assume that my faith must be huge. Actually, it's the other way around. It's not my faith in God, but His faith in me, that has enabled me to accomplish so much since Mark died. Our family couldn't have made it through our grief without God.

Every family needs a faith life. In good times and tough times, your faith can be a source of foundation, guidance, strength, and comfort.

Building a Foundation of Faith for Your Family

The main thing is to keep the main thing, the main thing.
Stephen R. Covey, American author

Is he alone who has courage on his right hand and faith on his left hand?
Charles Lindbergh (1902–1974), American aviator

Where there is FAITH, there is LOVE; Where there is LOVE; there is PEACE; Where there is PEACE; there is GOD; Where there is GOD; there is BLISS.
Sri Sathya Sai Baba, Indian spiritual leader

W hen building a house, if you don't get the foundation right, it doesn't matter how much you spend on the fancy windows, granite counters or imported roof tiles — eventually it's going to fall apart. Repairing a foundation is one of the toughest jobs in the construction industry. It is far cheaper and easier to get it done right the first time.

It's the same with building your family's faith. Building a strong foundation of faith is easier when your children are young than when you're trying to straighten out wayward teenagers a few years later. It's never too early to start building their faith.

ᔭᦂᕵ

Sometimes parents tell me that they don't want to brainwash their kids by teaching them one faith style. They prefer to let their children grow up and pick a faith when they are adults. That's risky thinking.

When Mark was dying in the hospital, I didn't have time to teach him who God was and the particulars of our faith. It brought me a lot of comfort knowing I had brought him and Amy to services every week and they knew the foundations of our faith. As you read in Chapter 2, his relationship with God gave him peace and comfort when he was in the hospital and as he passed over, too.

Bear in mind, just because you bring your children up in your faith doesn't guarantee that they will practice it as adults. They may even walk away from their faith completely. Hopefully, they will come back to a faith life in their later years, even if it isn't the same one they left.

Guidance

When we can't piece together the puzzle of our own lives, remember the best view of a puzzle is from above. Let Him help put you together.
Amethyst Snow-Rivers, writer

Most people wish to serve God — but only in an advisory capacity.
Unknown

I read about a mother who was preparing pancakes for her two sons, Andrew, age 5, and Steven, age three. The boys began to fight over who would get the first pancake. Their mother saw an opportunity for a moral lesson, so she said, "If Jesus were here, He would say, 'Let my brother have the first pancake. I can wait.'" Andrew turned to his younger brother and said, "Steven, you be Jesus."

When your family shares a faith, it can give you guidance when you need to make decisions, both big and small. It may be what to do with an unexpected tax refund or whether you spend your next vacation serving others or pampering yourselves. Sharing a faith is like you're using the same compass.

This book, and the rest of the Hug Your Kids Today project, is a response to my faith. I left a successful writing, speaking and consulting business because I felt God ask me to walk away. It was only after I did that He revealed this project to me. When I was running my company, this project never even crossed my mind. Now I can't imagine any other work.

Many people say I showed a lot of courage to follow His call. I say I would have required even more courage to ignore it. Can you imagine me telling God, "Sorry, I'm not interested?" or "I think my idea is better than Yours?" Not me.

Strength and Comfort

Faith supplies staying power... Anyone can keep going when the going is good, but some extra ingredient is needed to keep you fighting when it seems that everything is against you.

Dr. Norman Vincent Peale (1898–1993), American author

Fear can keep us up all night long, but faith makes one fine pillow.

Philip Gulley, American author, in his book, *Home Town Tales*

There is nothing that wastes the body like worry, and one who has any faith in God should be ashamed to worry about anything whatsoever.

Mahatma Gandhi (1869–1948), Indian philosopher

As a working parent, you know that it takes strength to make your life work when things are going smoothly. However, it's when something goes awry that it can take more strength than you've got on your own to keep the wheels from flying off your bus. A sudden diagnosis of cancer, heart problems in a loved one or an Enron-type surprise from your employer has wiped out many families, both financially and emotionally. Challenging times are when God's strength and comfort can make the difference between making it through and losing it all.

In Rabbi Harold Kushner's book, *When Bad Things Happen to Good People*, he says that when tough times hit, if you don't have faith, your strength will eventually run out. However, with faith, God continues to refill your strength, both spiritually and physically, so it doesn't run out. That was our family's experience, too.

For example, while God comforted me spiritually in my grief, He sent five neighborhood ladies to care for me and my family physically: Katherine Hoffman, Cathy Karr, Kathy Mudge, Leslie Newcomb, and Sherise Smith. These women were the helping hands, listening ears, wise mouths, soft shoulders and busy feet I needed to survive. My brother also called me every week or two as my heart mourned and healed. I would not be where I am today without the strength and comfort they, God and others provided.

Devin's Story — Putting Our Faith into Action

Everyone can be great because everyone can serve.
Dr. Martin Luther King, Jr. (1929–1968), American civil rights leader

We can all be angels to one another. We can choose to obey the still small stirring within, the little whisper that says, 'Go. Ask. Reach out. Be an answer to someone's plea. You have a part to play. Have faith.' We can decide to risk that He is indeed there, watching, caring, cherishing us as we love and accept love. The world will be a better place for it. And wherever they are, the angels will dance.
Joan Wester Anderson, American author

Rather than preaching to you about the importance of faith, let me tell you our story of Devin's adoption, which occurred against tremendous odds. You can draw your own conclusions. It contains all the elements I've mentioned: foundation, guidance, strength, and comfort. It's our faith put into action.

About six months after Mark died, I thought: *I've got to finish raising a boy.* This idea was so strong that I wrote it down.

I wasn't sure what I was supposed to do next. Amy was now seven years old and I was in my early 40s. For a variety of reasons, adopting a young boy was our family's best option. I wasn't trying to replace Mark; no one could, but Amy was miserable as a sudden only child.

There was just one big problem: Ron was completely against adopting. He said he was too afraid of losing another son. Undeterred, I started visiting some adoption agencies but no one would talk to me after they learned my husband wasn't on board with my plans.

I spent about a year trying to persuade my husband, with no luck. Then I asked God what He wanted me to do. I felt Him.tell me to wait.

Not long after, a woman I'd met only briefly asked me in the parking lot after church one Sunday, "Are you still interested in adopting a little boy?" She explained that she'd recently been at a sports event when a lady stood up and announced, "Does anybody know anyone who wants to adopt a little boy?" My friend said that she did.

The first woman said, "The only problem is, he's not an infant and most people want an infant."

My friend said, "The funny thing is, the family I'm thinking of specifically does not want an infant."

We learned the boy's name was Devin. He had just turned three years old. His birth mother was in jail. He was living with a senior couple and the elderly gentleman was in poor health.

A few weeks after we talked to the couple on the phone, we met them and Devin at a fast-food restaurant in the town they lived in, about 200 miles from us. Devin had big, brown curls; he was really cute. We watched him for about an hour. He played with some other little boys but he didn't pay much attention to us.

In contrast, Amy watched him for just a minute or two and exclaimed, "He's the one!" a line from the Disney movie *Beauty and the Beast*. Just as in the movie, where the clock is declaring that Belle is the one who's come to break the spell, Amy hoped Devin would break our spell of loneliness.

Breaking the Spell or Breaking Our Hearts?

Love is letting go of fear.

Unknown

fter meeting Devin, Ron's heart began to soften. We hired one of the top adoption lawyers. We learned this little boy wasn't legally available to adopt and his birth mother would not give up her parental rights. We asked our lawyer to explore our options. Devin visited with us a few times over the next six months. Soon he was living with us full time.

While he was still three years old, weighing less than 30 pounds, we had to give him up at the end of November. His birth mother was going to be released from jail. I did not want to risk legal complications.

His birth mother had no housing, transportation, money, or income. I had to pack him a bag of belongings that she could carry. Winter was coming; he needed clothes that were heavy enough to keep him warm in case they had to sleep under a bridge, but not so nice that she might sell them. It was hard to feel thankful that Thanksgiving.

The day before he left, a few friends came to our home and our minister led us in praying for this little boy's protection. My prayer was not necessarily that he be returned to our family, but I urgently prayed that he be kept safe and unharmed in any way. It was only with God's strength that I could let him go.

The next day, I had the tough job of driving Devin two hours away to a drop-off point with no plan of ever seeing him again.

After Devin was gone, I often went outside at night, looked up at the sky and shook my finger at God. I told Him, "You made this little boy, not me, and now You're responsible for him. He needs Your protection. It's Your responsibility to keep him safe."

I don't know why I thought God needed reminding, but I knew He was big enough to take a little finger shaking and yelling from this mother bear. The boy was like my little cub and I intended to do everything in my power to keep him safe, even at the risk of upsetting God.

Goodbye Devin. Pastor Bill Woolsey (standing) reading the Bible at Devin's send-off. Ron and Amy are on the right.

We continued our legal battle for Devin. At one point, when Ron and I had to make some tough decisions, I secluded myself in the bathroom outside our adoption lawyer's office to pray. I squatted down because the floor was too dirty to kneel on, and I prayed for God's guidance. I soon felt so peaceful that I almost felt like I was floating. I felt His soft, loving words, and gentle touch.

Less than a year later, we beat the long legal odds and adopted Devin into our family. It took two difficult lawsuits with five lawyers involved (four on our payroll.) Three years after Mark died, I started to finish raising a boy, just like the message I'd written down almost two years prior.

We were so thankful that throughout Devin's life, God protected this little boy. Despite all the dangerous circumstances he'd been through, which I won't go into, not a hair on his head had ever been harmed. Then God made a way for Devin to have a permanent family. To me, our son's story of protection and adoption is as amazing as the parting of the Red Sea.

Welcome to the family, Devin! From left, Amy, Devin and Ron.

Just two months after we adopted Devin, I wrote a letter to the editor at *BusinessWeek* that resulted in their creating the *Savvy Selling* column just for me in their online magazine. When you consider that even though I was a sales expert, my entire prior writing experience was the children's school newsletters, I believe that this huge opportunity was a thank-you gift from God for my faithfulness throughout Devin's adoption process.

SUMMARY

Developing and practicing your family's faith life will give them a firm foundation, guidance, strength, and comfort. Our adoption of Devin was an example of our family's faith in action.

Action Items

❶ If you're not practicing a faith regularly as a family, consider starting.

❷ Adopt a child (just kidding — or maybe not)

HUGS FROM MICHELLE'S FRIENDS

These "hugs" are from my friends who are experts in sales, religion, leadership, software, faith, and translating — from Utah to North Carolina.

Mark Hunter, Nebraska

Sales speaker and father of two college-aged children

I volunteer to help with our church's high school youth group. What I've found is that many of today's teenagers are lonely and under an incredible amount of peer pressure. Every day, they encounter situations that challenge their ethics and moral standards. Through my experiences, I have seen how faith can make a difference in their lives.

When a teenager does not have a faith they can anchor themselves to, they become much more susceptible to allowing themselves to be shaped by society, rather than helping shape it. As I've watched students move into adulthood, it is amazing to see how those who are grounded in their faith become productive adults much sooner than those who don't have faith.

This is not to say their lives are always easier. On the contrary, I've watched many struggle with significant challenges but, without exception, I've watched them deal with adversity and not let it derail their lives. In today's world, a child growing up without a strong faith is like a boxer going into a match with one arm tied behind his or her back. Having a faith life is that powerful.

Elaine McCalip, Texas

Bible study teacher and mother of a grown son

When Michelle came sweeping into my classroom on that cold, January day many years ago, coffee sloshing out of her thermos and anger, confusion, and hurt sloshing out of her deeply grieving soul, I quickly realized God was going to be changing both our lives by our interactions.

Wouldn't you know, our studies that semester concerned the tough questions people ask about our faith and trusting God! Over our years of Bible studies together, I've learned a lot from God and Michelle and, believe me, I spent a lot of time asking for His help as I tried to help her! The cool thing is that, in the challenge of our passionate and often heated discussions, I experienced how, if we ask for His help and rely on Him, God truly does lead us through all things.

Melody Salisbury, North Carolina

Michelle's childhood friend since seventh grade, mother of four children and stepmother of two adult children

One day as I was being wheeled into emergency surgery, I felt very alone and desperately wished that a loved one had been allowed to walk with me and hold my hand. I asked God to send someone to comfort me. He sent Himself. I immediately felt His hand in mine as I lay in the holding area just outside the surgery room door.

His comforting presence has continued. When my 47 year old father was diagnosed with cancer and he died 6 weeks later, while I was expecting my first child, God was there with me. When my first three children all struggled with serious illnesses, hospitalizations, and surgeries, God was there. When I traveled to Russia to adopt my fourth child, God was right there with me.

Later when I found myself single-parenting four children, two of which were strong-willed teenage boys, He was there, providing and caring for our needs in incredible ways that only He could do.

Shortly after my second son left for college, I was diagnosed with breast cancer that had metastasized. God's loving arms carried me as I underwent surgeries, hospitalizations, chemotherapy and radiation treatments. He comforted the boys when they were away at college as well as the two little ones at home with me.

He was also there when I walked down the aisle to marry a dear man who loved me and my children, even while I was fighting breast cancer. God has been with us as together we parent six children. Ten weeks ago when I sat in the ambulance as my husband was rushed to the hospital while having multiple heart attacks, God held my hand again. As I stood next to my sweetheart and agonizingly watched as he flat-lined and was gone, God heard my cry once more and mercifully brought him back to us.

Life isn't easy, and God didn't promise that it would be. However, He has promised that He would be there with us every step of the way. I have experienced the truth of His promises. Psalm 9:10b "You, Lord, have never forsaken those who seek you."

Mark Sanborn, Colorado
Author and speaker on leadership, and father of two school-aged boys

One way I help to build my sons' faith life is to pray with them before school. We pray for protection, a fun day of learning and we express gratitude for our family and our many blessings. I like to pray individually with each of the boys and make sure I have physical contact as we pray.

Susan Clark, Texas
Business owner and author on software, and mother of two college-aged sons

Here is an example of our faith helping one of my children. When my son was in the first grade, I found him crying one night because he couldn't visualize how to create a pop-up book for a class project. It was uncharacteristic for him to be so emotional about anything. I sat beside him on the bed and began to encourage him, telling him how smart he was and that I knew he would figure it out. However, nothing seemed to calm his near-hysterical crying.

Finally in desperation, I suggested that we pray about it. (Why is it that so often we only remember to ask for God's help as a last resort?) As we each silently prayed, I asked God to give me the words I needed to better explain the concepts he was trying to grasp.

Suddenly my son's whimpering ceased and he sweetly announced that he knew just what he needed to do the next day. Then he promptly fell asleep.

Once again, God had spoken to me through my little guy to remind me that I wasn't supposed to solve all my son's problems. My job was to let him learn to depend on God's guidance, even in the little things like making a pop-up book.

Christopher Hurtado, Utah

Owner of a translation company and father of eight children

Even though I have eight children, run a business and am a full-time student, no matter how busy I am I make it a point to have dinner with my family every night. As a student, this has meant changing our dinnertime almost every semester. As an entrepreneur, this has meant walking away from business opportunities at a significant loss of income.

After dinner every night, I lead my wife and children in singing hymns, memorizing scriptures, and praying together. Then I read the little ones an "upside down" story (as our family calls it), which means I hold a storybook of their choosing in front of me and read it to them upside down. Next, I usually tuck in either my son or the girls, after praying with them individually.

In the morning, my wife and I get up at 6:00 a.m. to read scriptures and pray with our older children before I take them to school. Upon returning from dropping them off, I usually have breakfast with my wife and younger children before I leave for work or school. However, before I walk out the door, I make it a point to hug my wife and children every day. This combination of faith and love gives my children the foundation to be happy and successful, both today and the rest of their lives.

CHAPTER 9

When you're too busy for your family, you're too busy.
— Thelma Wells, American speaker

You will never "find" time for anything. If you want time, you must make it.
— Charles Bruxton

*Time is too slow for those who wait, too swift
for those who fear, too long for those who grieve,
too short for those who rejoice,
but for those who love, time is eternity.*
— Henry Van Dyke (1852–1933), American writer

KEY LESSON #5:
Hug Your Kids Every Day

Hugging your kids is like brushing your teeth. If you only brush your teeth once a month, even if you do a fantastic job, it won't keep them from rotting out and you won't impress your dental hygienist on your next visit to the dentist.

The same idea applies to hugging your kids. Getting in the habit of hugging your kids every day will give you the peace of mind you want, with less guilt, worry, and stress.

I know that in a perfect world, you'd hug your kids several times a day — but you have work and a hundred other pressures that cry out for your time, too. As publisher Malcolm Forbes, Sr. once said, "There is never enough time, unless you're serving it."

If you're like most working parents I talk to, everyone wants more from you — your boss wants more, your customers or co-workers want more, your children and spouse want more — yet there are still only 24 hours in the day. This can produce frustration, a lack of focus and exhaustion that ultimately result in burnout, hardly the foundation for a successful career or a happy life.

✿❀✿

However, good parenting can't wait until you make your sales quota or empty your in-box. I couldn't live with myself today if I hadn't spent the time with Mark that I did. Did I give up most evening networking meetings? Yes. Did I miss a lot of weekend relationship-building functions? Yes. Did I skimp on getting to know my colleagues at after-work dinners? Yes.

Would I do it the same way again? Yes! Loving your kids can't wait until you have time in your schedule. Go hug them now, and tomorrow, too!

Daily Hugs — Building Love Habits

I love hugging. I wish I was an octopus, so I could hug ten people at a time.
Drew Barrymore, American actress

A hug is a great gift — one size fits all, and it's easy to exchange.
Unknown

Years ago, my children and I visited the George Ranch Historical Park in Richmond, Texas, for the Texian Market Days. There were historical reenactments, tours, and booths with folk life demonstrations. One of the booths had signs all over it that said, "We Don't Rent Pigs."

Like a sucker, I asked them why they didn't rent pigs. The actor replied with a straight face, "Because they never come back in the same condition we rented them." Hugging your kids every day will also change them — and it will change you, too.

❦

One of the best ways to increase the love in your family is to start habits of love. As you read earlier, Alan's love habit was to hug his daughter three times a day. In our family, whenever we part, either in person or when we're hanging up on the phone, our last words are always, "I love you."

Another habit is when a member of my family walks in the door, I always say, "Welcome home." My friend, speaker Tammy Ingraham, says, "When your family comes home, let it be the best part of their day. Let everything about your house say to them, 'Relax, you're home now.'"

Develop your own love habits, ones that work for you and your schedules. You know it takes 21 days to make a habit, so do whatever it takes to hug them consistently for 21 days in a row. You might program your hugs into your calendar, cell phone, or PDA or put a note on your refrigerator. Soon, your good intention will become a routine, and eventually, a habit.

Here's a story from Lisa Richeson, the mother of a boy in Mark's third-grade class, about a daily love habit that I had with Mark:

I'll always remember Michelle telling me her son always kissed her goodbye each day at school before going into his class. I thought, jealously, that perhaps she was not being completely truthful. Then one day, I saw it. Mark was calling out after kissing her, "Goodbye Mom, I love you." But she didn't hear him. Most children (or adults, even) at this point would have stopped. But Mark called out even louder, "Mom. I love you!" I will never forget it.

The Relativity of Time

Each day of our lives we make deposits in the memory banks of our children.

Charles R. Swindoll, American preacher

Watches are so named as a reminder — if you don't watch carefully what you do with your time, it will slip away from you.

Drew Sirtors, writer

I took Amy to a Starbucks coffee shop not long ago, and she ordered her favorite drink — a white mocha latte. She asked them for red sugar sprinkles. They told her the sprinkles were only available seasonally, but that day she was in luck; they had sprinkles. She was so happy; she skipped out of the store.

This story reminds me of how the value of things is relative for kids. She was more thrilled by the free sprinkles, than by the $5 I paid for her latte.

The beauty of a hug is it's like sprinkles on a latte. It may only take a minute, yet that minute may matter more than quietly sitting next to your kids for several hours while watching a movie or sports event. That's how time is relative when it comes to love. Relativity is great news for working parents.

Show Up

The bad news is time flies. The good news is you're the pilot.
Michael Altshuler, American author

Time is free, but it's priceless. You can't own it, but you can use it. You can't keep it, but you can spend it. Once you've lost it you can never get it back.
Harvey Mackay, American businessman

oody Allen said that 80% of success is showing up. When your kids are performing, whether it's a sports game or a dance recital, show up. While merely showing up at your children's event won't guarantee a successful, loving relationship, it is a prerequisite.

Show up even if the events are boring to you. It matters to your children and that makes it important. You might get to witness a priceless moment, one that the clearest retelling or video tape just can't capture, but that you talk about as a family for years later.

I admit: I'm a lousy spectator. It's hard for me to watch events, even when my kids are involved. I go anyway. I remember the first time Mark made a basket during an official basketball game. He was so proud; his face lit up the whole gym. Other moms still talk about it. I wouldn't trade the biggest sale I ever made for the memory of that moment.

꼬〇꼬

One of Ron's fondest memories of Mark's last year is when Ron gave a program on electricity for Mark's class. Ron created a booklet of facts and games about electricity, and built an elaborate display to show how electricity worked. I remember how proud Mark was the afternoon after his dad had presented to his class.

Show up. Your kids need hugs for "Good luck," "Congratulations" or "Maybe next time."

Time is the New Money

Time is life's money so be careful how you use it.
Tammy Ingraham, American speaker

If money is how we keep score in business, time spent with our loved ones is how we keep score in life.
Michelle Nichols

Over 200 years ago, Benjamin Franklin said, "Time is money" but now that's obsolete. Time is now more valuable than money because no matter how rich you are, you still have only 24 hours in your day. Not even Richard Branson or Oprah has 25 hours in his or her day.

In addition, time is like lettuce; it is perishable. An hour wasted at the office can never be recovered, whereas a dollar borrowed can be replaced by another dollar. That's why family time is more valuable than you can calculate in mere dollars and cents.

Be careful about who gets your time and how much. I keep timers in my office and around my home to help me be more careful about how much time I spend on tasks.

∽o∾

Here's my favorite joke about time and money:

A man trying to understand the nature of God asked him: "God, how long is a million years to you?"

God answered: "A million years is like a minute."

Then the man asked: "God, how much is a million dollars to you?"

And God replied: "A million dollars is like a penny."

Finally, the man asked: "God, could you give me a penny?"

And God said, "In a minute."

The Beatles Were Right — Money Can't Buy Me Love

Money often costs too much.

Ralph Waldo Emerson (1803–1882), American writer

Make money your god and it will plague you like the devil.

Henry Fielding (1707–1754), English dramatist

There is nothing wrong with men possessing riches. The wrong comes when riches possess men.

Rev. Billy Graham, American evangelist

oney is not the root of all evil. It's the love of money that is the root of all evil. In fact, John Wesley, a famous theologian, once said:

Earn all you can

Save all you can.

Give all you can.

That's three-quarters of a pretty good life goal. Of course, I'd add: Love all you can.

Put money in its proper place in your life. Money is a tool; it's your slave, and you are the master. I love the story about the rich man who got permission to bring a suitcase of whatever he wanted to Heaven with him. He decided to bring gold bricks. When he got there, people asked him, "Why did you bring paving stones?"

We came into this life with nothing and we will go out the same way. Everything we have is really on loan to us, to use or give away. When Mark died, he left with nothing, except a heart full of love.

To Disneyland (or Detroit or Denmark) We Go

We hit the sunny beaches where we occupy ourselves keeping the sun off our skin, the saltwater off our bodies, and the sand out of our belongings.
Erma Bombeck (1927–1996), American humorist

A vacation is what you take when you can no longer take what you've been taking.
Earl Wilson (1907–1987), American gossip columnist

My friend Steve calls vacations "forced family fun," but at least his family is having fun together. No matter what your schedule or financial situation is, get away with your family at least once a year. It creates stories and bonds you can't achieve any other way.

Don't wait for the perfect time to go on vacation with your family, because it will never come. Time rolls by, your kids grow up and eventually, we all lose our health and vigor. I had a very tight deadline to write this book and right in the middle was my children's spring break. I walked my talk — and we went on a four-day vacation in San Francisco. If I can do it, you can too.

I know a woman who put off buying a plush vacation retreat until she could afford it. By the time she'd saved the money, her kids were grown up and they didn't want to go with her because they had jobs and interests of their own. She regretted not buying a less-expensive unit ten years earlier, when she and her children could have had a lot of fun together.

∽o∾

A few years ago, I bought a travel trailer, and now I love to drive my kids around the country. We see the sites and visit friends and relatives, but mostly, we just hang out together.

Amy, a typical teenager, didn't want to go last year. However, by the end of the first day on the road she told me, "Mom, I love going on these trips. You haven't once told us, 'Hurry up, I have 42 things to do,' like you always do at home." (I admit, I cringed.)

In my office, I have pictures of us on our travels. They motivate me to work faster so I can get us back on the road to make more memories.

When you come home from one vacation, book the next one. I have never heard someone regretting taking their family on vacation. It may require juggling your family's schedules, but it's always worth it.

Girls (and Guys) Just Want to Have Fun!

I'm too busy to have a life.
A tired mom

We're not here for a long time, we're here for a good time.
Bob Parsons, American businessman

"Girls Just Want to Have Fun," the song by Cyndi Lauper, was a hit not just because of the catchy beat, but also because it's true. Of course, it's just as true for men. We all have an inner drive for fun.

Yet if you're like many working parents, you put "have fun" near the bottom of your priority list, maybe right after "have root canal." Then, like a beach ball held underwater for too long, your desire for fun comes shooting up to the surface and won't be ignored until you've bought a new Porsche or had $40,000 of plastic surgery.

∽o∾

No matter how efficient you strive to be, you were not the proto-type for a computer. Whether you crave a manicure or a round of golf with your friends, you need some fun in your schedule. You are not a machine; you are better. You can create, imagine — and most impor-tantly, you can love.

Pleasure is not selfish. If you know anyone who's lost 100 pounds, they didn't do it solely eating carrot sticks and watercress. Successful long-term diets allow dieters an occasional sweet, too. The same con-cept applies to you, so have some fun and enjoy it!

SUMMARY

Develop daily love habits so you hug your kids *every* day. Show up for your children's events, even if your schedule says you're busy and you think watching is boring. Time is more valuable than money. Go on vacations and have fun throughout the year.

Action Items

❶ Start a program to hug your kids and spouse every day for at least 21 days in a row.

❷ Schedule your next family vacation.

❸ Schedule something that's fun for you to do in the next week.

HUGS FROM MICHELLE'S FRIENDS

These "hugs" represent men and women who are experts in sales, magazine publishing, software, marketing, book publishing, wealth management, and oncology — from Nevada to New York. Read 'em and reap.

Jill Konrath, Minnesota

Author, sales expert, and mother of two college-aged children

When my kids were little, I used the drive time to daycare each morning to connect with them. We frequently played the "How About" pretend game. For example, the minute my son hopped in the car, he'd say, "How about you be the bad guy and I'll be the cop?" He liked to try out various roles but when my daughter played this game, she was always Dorothy from *The Wizard of Oz*. For the next 25 minutes, we stayed in our roles, weaving a fantasy story in which we were the main characters.

It was great fun for all of us — great for creativity, and great for sharing our time together. I know that the daily ritual of our morning pretend games helped them feel confident, special, and most importantly, loved, all day long, until we were back together again that night.

Katrina Katsarelis, Texas

Publisher of six magazines and mother of two teenage children

One of the ways I show my love for my family every day is I write love messages on their bedroom and bathroom mirrors using whiteboard markers. For example: "Somebody loves you!", "You are loved!" and "You Are My Son-Shine." One time, I decorated my teenage daughter's car with hearts, kisses, and "I love you" messages. She was so surprised and touched; she left it on for days.

Craig Klein, Texas

Owner of a software company and father of two young children

I show my love to my kids by teaching them to make good choices. I respect them when we're discussing their responsibilities. I try to communicate why something is important in a way they can understand. I explain the trade-offs and consequences. Then I ask them if they understand. (From my sales training, I've learned to confirm my "customer" heard what I said.) Finally, I give them the responsibility to choose. They feel powerful when they get to choose and when undesired consequences occur, they understand and learn from them.

It would be easier to just tell my kids what to do but I feel it's important to teach them how to choose well. They have a lifetime of choices ahead of them and I want them to learn to make good choices. After all, they may be choosing my old folks' home someday!

Maureen Blandford, Ohio

Sales and marketing consultant, and mother of two teenage daughters

With two daughters in junior high, I've learned that puberty combines the best of times and the worst of times. While their worlds are exploding with new knowledge, discoveries and fun every day, their hormones are wreaking havoc with them and their peers. Navigating new temptations, mean girls, and increased schoolwork is so much easier in an atmosphere of confidence and good cheer. Daily doses of hugs give my girls just that.

I've found that just as important as getting plenty of sleep and water, a healthy diet, and exercise, my girls need love and hugs to see them through the day. That's why I've made showing my daughters that I love them and believe in them a part of my daily regimen.

Jeb Blount, Florida

Sales speaker, book publisher, and father of a school-aged son

In December 2006, I made a goal to "be a better father and husband." The most specific thing I could think of to reach this goal was to eat dinner as a family a minimum of three times each week.

Unfortunately, we had each fallen into the habit of doing our own thing at dinnertime. It took some "selling" but I convinced them to turn off all entertainment during dinner — phones, TVs, video games, and computers. I'll admit, the first night was awkward. We just sat and stared at each other, secretly wishing that we could all go back to our old ways. However, we stuck with it and within a month, we had gotten in a rhythm of asking about each other's days, telling stories, laughing, and working together to make dinner and clean up after our meals.

Soon we were eating together about five nights a week. Over the next few months, we became closer; I learned about what was important to my son and I gave my wife the one thing she craved — my attention. A year later, instead of watching TV or playing video games, my son and I were playing basketball or going for bike rides after dinner. I hugged him more frequently, tucked him into bed more often, and enjoyed our time together more.

One of the best rewards from our increased time together was when my wife and I renewed our wedding vows in Hawaii for our 15-year anniversary. I feel I reached my goal of being a better father and husband, and I look forward to more good times together with my family in the years ahead.

Nadine Wong, New York

An executive director at Morgan Stanley Private Wealth Management and mother of two school-aged children

Besides spending quality time with my children, I teach them arts and crafts, such as jewelry making. They create earrings and necklaces, and either give them as gifts, or sell them to learn valuable business skills. Additionally, each night when I tuck them into bed, I tell them they are destined for greatness because of their hard work, kindness, determination and unique attributes. Then I tell them, "I love you," followed with a hug and kiss good night.

Dr. Tricia May, Nevada

Surgical oncologist and mother of three young children

It would be easy for me to carry my work home in my head, but when my workday is over, I make a conscious decision to leave my work at work. When I get home to my three precious little ones, I'm not "Dr. May," I'm just "Mommy."

I show my love to my children by physically getting down on their level so I can hear what's going on in their lives from their perspective. For instance, when we were reading a book with the poem about the five little monkeys jumping on the bed, as I got to the line, "Momma called the doctor and the doctor said, 'No more monkeys jumping on the bed,'" my daughter commented, "That's crazy! It's fun to jump on the bed."

I wanted to give her a speech about safety and following directions, but instead, I just laughed and appreciated that kids have a completely different perspective on life than the adults I work with every day.

I feel blessed and thank God that He has put me in this role at work to help others. I am a better mom because I get to give and help others at work. However, the best part of my day is when I get to go home and hug my kids and my husband.

PART 3

Your Next Step

Don't wait. The time will never be just right.
—Napoleon Hill (1883–1970), American author

CHAPTER 10

Talk doesn't cook rice.
— Chinese proverb

Small deeds done are better than great deeds planned.
— Peter Marshall, English author

Affirmation without action is the beginning of delusion.
— Jim Rohn, American speaker

Go Forth and Love Abundantly

Picture yourself sitting down, waiting for your youngest child's graduation or wedding to begin. The background music is playing as guests are being seated. You're probably thinking that he or she grew up so quickly. You begin to recall some key moments in his or her life — losing a first tooth, starting junior high, and going on a first date.

How do you feel? Do you feel contented that you showed your love to your children on a daily basis, with lots of hugs, snuggles, and time spent together? Or are you suddenly filled with remorse and regrets that you should have spent less time at work and more time with those who truly matter to you — and now it's too late? Your child is grown up and moving on to the next phase in his or her life, one where you play only a supporting role.

The time to make sure you have the first response, and not the second, is now. Feeling love in your heart and thinking loving thoughts in your mind don't impact your family. Only actions matter.

∽o∾

In sales, we say that nothing happens until somebody sells something. Salespeople can go to all the best sales classes, read all the latest sales books, talk to all the leading sales experts, but it's only once they start talking to prospective customers, that they begin making sales.

The same is true for all professions. Reports don't create themselves, products don't design themselves and patients don't cure themselves. It takes education plus action to achieve the results you want.

Mission: Hug Your Kids Today and Every Day

Imagine you are a rocket scientist. You've built your rocket and now it's launch time. Similarly, it's time to put everything you've learned in this book into action. Have you hugged your kids and your spouse today? Good. Repeat it every day until it's an established habit.

I've done my part. Now I'm giving you a push to start turning this information into results. Taking action, and enjoying the rewards, is up to you.

∽o∾

The main character in the book *Venus Envy* by Shannon McKenden said that regret is like if your life were to flash before your eyes, but it's not the life you lived but the life you could have lived. If you don't start today to hug your kids every day, there's a chance that some day down the line, you're going to regret that decision.

∽o∾

Taking action to hug your kids every day involves commitment and risk, but the rewards can be priceless. Here's an example of a priceless reward our family received from Mark.

On his last Valentine's Day, as a class assignment, Mark wrote a long poem called, "Honey I Love." All the verses had the same pattern and discussed how much he loved his computer, basketball, Nintendo 64, his bedroom light, reading, football, baseball, and the Olympics. The funniest verse was:

I like hockey.
I get ice wedgies from Genuine Jockey.
I hit a slapshot.
It goes in the net on the dot.
Honey, let me tell you that I love hockey.

But it's the last three verses that we treasure most.

I love my mom.
She worked hard to get me into Roy Gomm.*
She is really, truly crazy
But for me, she's never lazy.
Honey let me tell you how I love my mom.

I love my dad.
I think he's totally rad.
He coached me and the Cubs.**
When I fall off my bike, my hurt he rubs.
Honey, let me tell you how I love my dad.

I love Amy, my sister.
I wouldn't trade her for a blister.
I try to teach her everything I know.
She learns fast, not slow.
Honey, let me tell you how I love Amy, my sister.

* *his elementary school*
** *his Little League baseball team*

And Now He Calls Me "Mom"

To reach out to another is to risk involvement. To expose feelings is to risk exposing your true self. To place your ideas and dreams before a crowd is to risk their loss. To love is to risk not being loved in return, To live is to risk dying. To hope is to risk despair. To try is to risk failure. But risks must be taken because the greatest hazard in life is to risk nothing. The person who risks nothing, does nothing, has nothing, is nothing. He may avoid suffering and sorrow, but he cannot learn, feel, change, grow or live.

William Arthur Ward (1924–1994), American author

After all our hard work to adopt Devin, he threw me a curve ball on his adoption day. Since he'd never had a dad, he told my husband, "You can be my dad."

He'd never had a sister, so he told Amy, "You can be my sister."

However, since he remembered his birth mother, even though his memories were painful, he told me, "You can be Amy's mom."

Somehow, I was able to calmly say, "OK." I can't believe that I didn't let loose with, "Do you know what we went through for you?" followed by a long, impassioned rant. Instead, I felt in my heart that he'd accept me in his own time.

And now he calls me "Mom."

Love Abundantly and Fearlessly

I can accept failure; everyone fails at something. But I can't accept not trying.

Michael Jordan, American basketball superstar

Most people overestimate what they can accomplish in a year — and underestimate what they can achieve in a decade.

Anthony Robbins, American speaker

You may never know what results come of your action, but if you do nothing there will be no result.

Mahatma Gandhi (1869–1948), Indian philosopher

One day, while I was browsing in a party store, I realized that after all our family had been through, we were like the Disney character family, *The Incredibles*. I went to the party aisle and bought a four-pack of identical rings and masks with the *Incredible* logo.

When I got home, I secretly wrote a note to each family member:

Extreme, Very Big, Ultimate Tip-top Secret.

You, (name,) have been selected for a very special assignment. Please wear or carry the enclosed jewelry the rest of the day. At dinner, you will meet the other members of your team. They will have matching jewelry.

More will be revealed at dinner.

Until then, don't lose the ring or forget to . . . (some chore I am always nagging them about.) Sh-h-h-h-h!

I put each ring, mask, and note in a small gift bag and hid it in their lunches. Of course, at the end of the day, they couldn't wait to see what would happen next.

Why did I do this? To put the love I felt for my family into action.

❦

What if you reach out to hug someone you love and you get rebuffed? Maybe they won't meet you at the airport, accept your phone call, or otherwise respond to your overtures of love.

Hang in there. Keep reaching out and trying to love them. Until one of you takes your dying breath, keep trying.

Either they'll eventually accept, and your relationship is restored, or they never accept, and you still have the good feeling that you gave it your all. You won't be left with any regrets or "coulda', woulda', shoulda's."

∽o∼

Famous inventor Thomas Edison said, "We don't know a millionth of one percent about anything." That's .00000001%! Yet I hope I've convinced you of the importance of hugging your kids and your spouse, every day, starting today.

Final Thoughts

The way to get done is to get started.
Michelle Nichols

Someday, after mastering winds, waves, tides and gravity, we shall harness the energy of love; and for the second time in the history of the world, man will have discovered fire.
Pierre Teilhard De Chardin (1881–1955), French priest and paleontologist

Without love, what are we worth? Eighty-nine cents! Eighty-nine cents worth of chemicals walking around lonely.
Spoken by the character Hawkeye (played by Alan Alda) in the TV show
M*A*S*H, episode "Love Story."

It doesn't matter how good your intentions to love your family are or how passionately you feel them. What matters is putting them into action.

I once read that 90% of the time when you're faced with a decision, you know what to do. You're just afraid to do it.

- Step into love's spotlight — and hug.
- Hug first, fast and always.
- Hug like no one's watching.
- Do less. Hug more.
- Stop doing activities that won't matter next year.
- Start doing more activities that matter ten years from now.
- If you want a closer relationship with your loved ones, be easier to hug.
- Forget trying to be Super Dad or Super Mom.
- Hug your kids.
- Speak hugs.
- Write hugs.
- Think hugs.
- Spread hugs.
- Be hugs.
- Hug your kids today!

I wrote this poem in honor of Devin but it applies to all children.

If You Can Hug a Child, You Can Heal the World
By Michelle Nichols 2006

If you can hug a child, you can love that child.
If you can love a child, you can heal that child.
If you can heal a child, you can heal a family.
If you can heal a family, you can heal a nation.
If you can heal a nation, you can heal the world.
But first, you must hug a child.

As they say in Texas: You got it. Now get at it!

LOVE WINS.
—A bumper sticker.

CHAPTER 11

Even though it's my right, I ain't gonna take revenge.
And you wanna know why? Because you got a problem.
You got a problem with aggression. I don't know —
maybe you weren't hugged when you were a kid.

—Mobster Paul Vitti (played by Robert DeNiro) in the movie

Analyze This, after a fellow mobster tried to kill Paul and missed,

so now Paul has the right to kill him in return

Epilogue

What can I add to this book and my five key lessons?

Only a few more stories, but they all point back to the importance of loving your family every day.

I continue to believe "work-life balance" is a fool's errand. You can't balance work and life because there is no conversion rate between activities that are significant and those that merely "pay-the-bills."

Even if you love your work, and I hope you do, work pales in comparison to the joy and life significance derived from doing a good job raising your kids, and loving them and your spouse. If you don't believe this, you must have missed Chapter 3.

Yet work provides you with so many benefits besides your livelihood, including a sense of accomplishment, identity, and opportunities to create, contribute and lead.

I still believe that if you hug your kids and your spouse the first thing every day, you'll be happier, more contented and more productive the rest of the day — *and so will they.* Your laughter and good memories are bonuses.

OK, one more lesson.

Let It Be

Lord, grant me the serenity to accept the things I cannot change, the courage to change the things I can, and the wisdom to know the difference.
St. Francis of Assisi (1181–1226), Italian friar

Everybody has a little bit of Watergate in him.
Rev. Billy Graham, American evangelist

fter I gave a speech recently, a young gal came running up to me and asked me my secret for having had five jobs and starting four companies despite my personal challenges. She said she had lots of plans for her life too.

I'd never thought of this question before but my answer was, "Flexibility." I told her that to have the best that life offers, you need to be flexible about most things, and inflexible about a few things, like family, relationships, and personal integrity.

Before Mark died, I had firm plans of how I wanted my life to unfold. If something got in my way or slowed me down, I got frustrated. I was a model of inflexibility.

I've come to realize that sometimes random stuff happens. You can't line up all the dots in your life to make a logical pattern.

Now, I take my cue from the Beatles' song, "Let it Be." Speaker Joe Calloway phrases it, "Let it go." Golfers call it "play it where it lies." A generation prior, there was a popular song, "Que Sera, Sera (Whatever

Will Be, Will Be)."

Whatever phrasing works for you, using this attitude of flexibility can help you to accept and adapt when things don't go your way. It can even help you look for the opportunities in your new situation.

Family Update

ere's what our family is doing as of this writing.

Ron retired and our family moved back to Reno, Nevada, where we lived when Mark died. We love Reno because it offers a great business environment. It has four seasons, so we can ski in the winter, hike in the summer and enjoy a wide variety of entertainment year around.

We put up a Christmas tree this year, for the first time in nine years since Mark died. My kids didn't remember any of the ornaments but we all lit up when we turned on the lighted, decorated tree. It's another step in making our way back to "normal."

Cheese! Our family at the top of the mountain at Jackson Hole, Wyoming.

Ron spends his time volunteering at several local charities. He prepares our kids' lunches every night, quizzes Devin on his spelling words, and is teaching Amy to drive. He makes our family run smoothly.

೧∞ೖ

Amy is now a teenager. She's just half an inch short of six feet tall, with red hair. She plans to go to college and maybe even medical school. She still keeps her thoughts and secrets to herself. ("That's why they're called secrets, Mom," she tells me.) She likes "chick flicks" because she says they're the way life is supposed to be.

೧∞ೖ

Devin attends the same elementary that Mark and Amy did. In fact, he had Mark's teacher last year. He also plans to go to college but mostly, he looks forward to marrying a nice girl and having many children.

He has a special heart for animals of all types, from polar bears to salamanders. He has two pet frogs ("Mr. and Mrs. Harrison"), and one pet turtle named "James Pond."

For me, one of the great results of his adoption is its impact on future generations. Now he will probably marry better, they will most likely have more successful children, and they will probably marry better, and so on. By changing the course of his life, we affect many other lives in the future.

೧∞ೖ

As for me, after six years of being known as "Ms. BusinessWeek," I thought it would be hard to change my identity to "Ms. Hug Your Kids Today," but most days, it's easy.

One big change in me since Mark died is I am now fearless. I'm no longer scared of hearing "No" because I've lived through the ultimate "No" for any parent.

Nothing intimidates me, not even things I don't understand. For example, I heard that *BusinessWeek* was famous for their podcasts and even though I didn't have any idea what they were, I asked my editor at *BusinessWeek.com* if I could record some podcasts.

Four months later, he called me with the green light. I still didn't know what a podcast was but I told him I could start in a week. My next phone call was to a technical friend to ask, "What the heck is a podcast?"

The first guest I lined up was "Mr. Motivation" Zig Ziglar — what a thrill. I ultimately recorded 45 podcasts for *BusinessWeek.com,* until we lost our sponsor. I still get emails from subscribers asking me when I'm going to start recording them again.

∽∘∾

After I spent years trying to get my parents to apologize, I finally just decided to forgive them. We have a good relationship now and our family sees and calls them often. Life is too short to do otherwise.

Perhaps someday I will write a book on the power of forgiveness. For now, if you're struggling to forgive someone, here are three quotes that have really helped me:

> *He that cannot forgive others breaks the bridge over which he must pass himself; for every man has need to be forgiven.*
> Thomas Fuller (1608–1661), English historian

> *Forgiveness is unlocking the door to set someone free and realizing you were the prisoner.*
> Max Lucado, American author

> *The only thing harder than forgiveness is the alternative.*
> Philip Yancey, American author

In Closing

The highest compliment my children ever paid me came one night after Ron and I returned home from attending a social function. The house was quiet so I knew both children were asleep. There was a note taped to our bedroom door that said, "Mom, watch out. I'm sleeping on the floor next to your bed. Devin."

After all he had been through in his short life, that note told me that just being near my side of the bed, when I wasn't even home, made him feel safe. I felt like I'd been awarded the Mother's Medal of Honor.

∽o∾

Do we still miss Mark? Of course. There's not enough chocolate, wine, or other fun stuff in the world to fill that hole in our hearts, but we are happy and feel good about the meaningful lives we have created.

Humorist Erma Bombeck said, "When I stand before God at the end of my life, I would hope that I would not have a single bit of talent left, and could say, 'I used everything you gave me.'" Likewise, I hope when I'm in that situation, I won't have a single bit of love left and I can say, "I gave away every bit of love I had." If you'll put these five key lessons into practice, you can say the same, too.

Life is lived going forward but often only understood looking backward. I hope by me looking backward and sharing our story, you and your family will have happier lives going forward, filled with love, laughter and good memories.

Your children are incredibly special. No matter their age, size, abilities or temperament, they are worthy of love and celebration, just the way they are at this moment.

Now go hug your kids — and your spouse. Look for the positive in everything they do. Laugh as often as you can, develop your family's faith — and remember to hug them again tomorrow.

HUGS FROM MICHELLE'S BOOK CLUB

I love my book club. We represent a variety of occupations but we all share a love of reading and talking about good books. Instead of giving you a list of questions for your book club, I thought you'd like to hear what my book club thought about this book. Here are their "hugs."

Jennifer Lunt

Alternate public defender and mother of a grown daughter (who's also a lawyer)

This is a great book! It had the three qualities I look for in a book — it made me laugh, it made me cry, and it made me think.

Michelle took a tragedy and turned it into something positive, beneficial, and powerful. A simple idea — a hug! — can have an incredible impact. It made me wonder why we sometimes forget to hug. One of the first things an infant will do is hug. Who hasn't seen a toddler careen across a room and throw herself into a hug from a loved one?

Where exactly did we get the idea that we have outgrown hugs? Michelle's book made me realize that no one is too old for a hug.

Bonnie Saviers

Marketing coordinator for a public library system, mother of an adult daughter, and grandmother of two school-aged boys

I was a working mom back in the '70s when that was much less common than it is today. A book like *Hug Your Kids Today!* would have been invaluable to me back then, giving me reassurance that I wasn't a horrible, selfish person for working at a career I enjoyed. Michelle's tips would have helped me make the most of my precious time with my daughter who, by the way, grew up to be a wonderful young woman and a successful, happy working mom in her own right. I plan to buy my daughter her own copy of this fabulous book!

Lisa Dayton

Quilt artist and mother of two teenage boys

I don't normally read self-help books but this one had a chapter that was just what I needed to hear. My teenage son got a bad haircut yesterday. He was so upset about it that he stayed up all night and as a result, he missed a day of school today. He made a hurtful comment to me this afternoon that left me wondering if he was hormonal, rude or just testing me. I decided to ignore his behavior but for the next few hours, I questioned my decision.

Then I read Key Lesson #2 — *Carpe Kids,* and I felt validated, as if I did the right thing. I felt glad that I'd decided to turn the other cheek and not to engage with him.

If I hadn't read that chapter, I'd still be questioning my reaction to his behavior. This made a difference in how the rest of my day went. It made me more conscious of how I came across to everyone. I'm glad Michelle reminded me that we don't have to scrutinize every shortcoming of our children and we can focus instead on their positive traits.

The message that shines through in this book for everybody is you don't know how long any of us will live, so you should enjoy — and hug — your loved ones today.

Gail Burns

Project manager at a large utility company and mother of two school-aged children

I laughed and cried as I read this book. I appreciate that Michelle had the courage and ability to share her experiences with all of us. She inspired me to do a much better job of saving mementos, journaling, and scrap-booking going forward. The bigger lesson, of course, is to remember to show my love to my two sweet children and my wonderful husband every day.

Karen Ross

Community relations manager for a large utility

Although I don't have any children, this book drew me in. It is really about the universal message to love the people who are important to you and to remember to demonstrate that love every day.

The book also made me think of other universal themes, like loss and forgiveness. It's definitely not just for working parents, or even parents. It is a reminder to anyone who reads it to live and value each moment.

I'm still a newlywed, married less than two years to the man I know I am destined to spend the rest of my life with. This book reminded me of the depth of my own love for him. Many thanks to Michelle for reminding me to value and express this powerful gift.

Laura Walsh

A pricing manager at a large utility and single mom of a school-aged daughter

I loved this book because it made me stop and look at my own life. Given all the demands of work, home and my daughter, it is sometimes easy to lose focus. In this book, Michelle reminds me to see what really matters. Work can be like a sieve. I can keep pouring myself into it, but it never gets full or overflows.

My daughter, on the other hand, is like a solid vessel. She takes and stores all that I give her, both good and bad. Whatever I share with her becomes a part of who she is, now and in the future. Therefore, my top priority is to give her my best every day, even if it isn't easy.

Michelle also reminds me to lighten up and have more fun with my amazing daughter. I promise to do that too, but no cape or monster trucks for us!

Alissa Turner

Civil engineer and mother of a preschool-aged daughter

Hug Your Kids Today! struck many chords with me but let me share one that covers three generations of hugs.

When I was growing up, my mother — third out of a family of eleven children — was never very affectionate and she was uncomfortable giving or receiving hugs. This bugged me, so for the last two years of high school, I consciously gave my mom a big hug and a kiss and told her I loved her every day before I left for school and she left for work. It wasn't easy and it took a lot of perseverance, but by the time I graduated from high school and was ready to go away to college, she was able to give a reciprocal hug and an "I love you, too," and I knew she really meant it.

I'm now the proud mother of a beautiful daughter and from the day she was born I have showered her daily with hugs, kisses, and whispers of "I love you." She is growing up to be a wonderful, outgoing child who gives hugs on a whim and tells those she is close to that she loves them.

Here's the best part of the story: The first time my daughter told my mother that she loved her, my mother excitedly called to tell me about it. She spoke as if it was the first time anyone had ever told her they loved her! I was so happy to hear the joy in my mother's voice.

Shauna Adams

Manager of major projects for a large utility and mother of two adult children

I laughed, I cried, and I blew my nose more than a few times! I am so grateful I read this book because it reminded me of the important stuff and validated my thinking that success means a happy family and not just a fat paycheck.

Key Lesson #3, "When All Else Fails, Laugh," made me think of the time I stripped the wallpaper off the bathroom walls to prep them for paint. Soon after, my son and his cousin decided to draw on the walls. Instead of getting mad, I put a set of markers in the bathroom and let all who wanted to have free expression on the walls. His friends all thought it was great. It was quite colorful and it stayed that way for many years.

This book reaffirmed my commitment to be there for my kids when they want to talk, even if it's not convenient for me. My son is now grown. He's a "night owl" and often calls me when I am asleep. I am thankful for his calls at any time. I might be sleepier the next day but it's worth it to hear his voice.

Donna Smit

Project coordinator at the local water company and mother of two grown sons

I think Michelle's book is a lesson for us all to remember to tell our loved ones every day, "I love you!"

Here are three ideas that struck me while reading the book: how in times of despair, the simple things like baking brownies can mean so much; I loved her drawing titled, "Between Life and Death, Insert Love" (brilliant!); and good huggers are the best people in life. I enjoyed reading her husband's reflections, too.

Maizie Pusich

Chief deputy public defender and mother of two school-aged children

A hug of congratulations and gratitude to Michelle for writing *Hug Your Kids Today!* It reminded me of the power of a simple hug. I've used hugs to tell my children: "I am proud of you," "My thoughts and prayers are with you," "Please forgive me," "I've missed you," and "You mean every-thing to me." Hugs are truly one size fits all situations.

As a public defender, I deal with a lot of people who didn't get the hugs or love they needed from their parents when they were growing up. This book reminds me that it's always a good time to hug my chil-dren and tell them again how dear they are to me.

Lee Harris

Lighting designer and single mother of two teenagers

My two kids couldn't be more different. My son has always been the hugger in the family, knocking me down with his running hugs when I picked him up from preschool. Now that he's a teenager, I have to seek out his hugs. Michelle shows us how to do that and how valuable this practice is.

My daughter was always more protective of "her space" and didn't seek out hugs. After she had a difficult time transitioning into high school, we saw a counselor and she recommended hugs! It took my daughter some getting used to hugs but now she hugs freely and abundantly and is much happier.

As my children move through the challenging adolescent years, this book reminds me I need to keep trying to find ways to show my kids I love them in ways they can accept. My thanks to Michelle for writing this book and teaching us that sometimes the complex issues of balancing work and family can be solved with a sense of humor about ourselves and our kids, faith, and lots of hugs!

Resources

Web Resources

The project behind this book is **www.HugYourKidsToday.com**

The Compassionate Friends, an organization for families who have had a child die at any age and for any reason. **www.thecompassionatefriends.com**

Beautiful Ready-to-Frame Display of the 5 Key Lessons

Download for no charge: **www.HugYourKidsToday.com**

Book and Magazine Resources

This Is How We Do It: The Working Mother's Manifesto by Carol Evans

Working Mother magazine

The Bible

Fatherhood by Bill Cosby

What Do You Really Want for Your Children? by Dr. Wayne Dyer

Stop Screaming at the Microwave by Mary Lo Verde

Any book by:

Erma Bombeck, especially *I want to Grow Hair, I want to Grow Up, I want to Go to Boise*

Dr. Leo Buscaglia, especially *Love: What Life is All About*

Patsy Clairmont, especially *Normal is Just a Setting On Your Dryer*

Robert Fulghum, especially *All I Really Need to Know I Learned in Kindergarten*

Rabbi Harold Kushner, especially *When Bad Things Happen to Good People*

Zig Ziglar, especially *Confessions of a Grieving Christian*

Acknowledgments

To paraphrase Hillary Clinton, "It takes a village to raise a book." Although many people helped my family through our journey and the writing of this book, these people deserve special mention:

Dave Balch, Jeb Blount, John and Virginia Bufkin, Ken Dwight, Frances Ennis, Rebecca Fox, Roger Franklin, Dr. Glen and Melinda Ginter, Ruben Gonzalez, Lee Harris, Katherine Hoffman, Regina Ives, Cathy Karr, Rennis and Bonna Kauffman, Nick Leiber, Stephie Mager, Joyce Margarce, Don and Betty Maynard, Phil and Lisa Maynard, Elaine McCalip, Kathy Mudge, Leslie Newcomb, Mike Price, Howard Putnam, Debbie Rasmassen, Shirley Rodriguez, Susan Schulte, Darcie Sims, PhD, Sherise Smith, and Carol and Paul Steffanni. Also, my book club members and other friends who took the time to write a "Hug" for you.

A special Thank You to:

Susan Holshouser Vice-President, and Pete Mack, Operations Manager, of Clear Channel Outdoor for creating the digital billboard art. They also donated digital billboards in Reno and led other cities to donate digital billboards on July 21, 2008.

Tony Brigmon, who wrote and produced the song "Hug Your Kids Today" and donated it to the project.

Robin Tanner of the Reno Technical Institute and her amazing Digital Video students who created the initial YouTube videos for this project. Thanks too to Karen Burns and Kia Crader for choreographing and organizing the students and their families from Fascinating Rhythm School of Performing Arts for a wonderful YouTube video. Thanks to Cassandra Hemsley for making the video.

Vicky Vaughn Shea, Rebekah Foster, Judy Vaughan, and Carleen Madigan Perkins for turning this sweat- and tear-stained manuscript into a beautiful book.

My dogs, Oreo and Penny, who sat at my feet and listened patiently as I read them each chapter. I think they want my next book to be "Hug Your Dogs Today."

About the Author
Michelle Nichols

Nationwide Event Creator – Michelle Nichols founded *National Hug Your Kids Day* (3rd Monday in July) and created the *Hug Your Kids Today* project. It will launch July 21, 2008 and continue year-around.

Speaker and Workshop Leader – Michelle speaks and gives workshops to corporate, industry, association and Christian audiences to help their working parent employees be more productive, happy, and successful. She has spoken on sales to groups from ten to five hundred. Her clients have included HP, Hibernia Bank, Clarica Insurance, ASAE, the National Ground Water Association, and the U.S. Postal Service.

She is a member of the prestigious National Speakers Association and the past Chair of the sales experts for NSA.

Columnist, Author, Podcast Host and CD Creator – Ms. Nichols is the author of more than 150 *Savvy Selling* columns and 45 podcasts published by *BusinessWeek.com*. *BusinessWeek* sent her work to more than 200,000 subscribers in 50 countries. She also published the *Idea Generation Guide* and wrote and recorded three sales CDs.

Hobbies and Interests – Michelle likes to bake chocolate chip cookies, grow tomatoes and roses, drive her trailer around the U.S. to visit friends and interesting sites, and of course, hug her family.

Proudest Accomplishment– Of all her accomplishments, Michelle is most proud to be the wife of Ron for over 20 years and the mother of Mark, Amy and Devin. She hugs them and loves them, every day.

Book Michelle to Speak at Your Next Event

To invite Michelle Nichols to speak, arrange for bulk book orders or for more information, call toll-free (877) 352-9684 / direct (775) 303-8201.

www.HugYourKidsToday.com / hugo@HugYourKidsToday.com

P.O. Box 34090, Reno, NV, 89533, USA

Quick Order Form

NOTE: If this is a library book, please make a COPY of this page.

Phone Orders: Call (877) 352-9684 toll-free or (775) 303-8201.

Email Orders: hugs@HugYourKidsToday.com

Online Orders: www.HugYourKidsToday.com. Click on SHOP.

Postal Orders: Hug Your Kids Today, Michelle Nichols, P.O. Box 34090, Reno, NV, 89533, USA.

Bulk Order or Fundraiser Discounts: We are happy to give discounts to orders of 5 copies placed at the same time. Please call (877) 352-9684 toll-free to discuss discounts.

❑ **Send me the free monthly "Hug Your Kids Today" newsletter.**

❑ **Contact me about having Michelle speak, train or consult.**

Name: _____

Address: _____

City, State, Zip: _____

Telephone: _____

Email address: _____

Cost of books: For orders up to 4 copies, books are $17.95 USD each. For orders of 5 or more books, call (877) 352-9684 or (775) 303-8201.

Sales tax: Please add 7.375% for books shipped to Nevada addresses.

Shipping by U.S. Postal Service:

U.S.: $4.00 for first book and $2.00 for each additional book

International: $9.00 for first book and $5.00 for each additional book

THANK YOU!

Quick Order Form

NOTE: If this is a library book, please make a COPY of this page.

Phone Orders: Call (877) 352-9684 toll-free or (775) 303-8201.
Email Orders: hugs@HugYourKidsToday.com
Online Orders: www.HugYourKidsToday.com. Click on SHOP.
Postal Orders: Hug Your Kids Today, Michelle Nichols, P.O. Box 34090, Reno, NV, 89533, USA.
Bulk Order or Fundraiser Discounts: We are happy to give discounts to orders of 5 copies placed at the same time. Please call (877) 352-9684 toll-free to discuss discounts.

❑ **Send me the free monthly "Hug Your Kids Today" newsletter.**
❑ **Contact me about having Michelle speak, train or consult.**

Name: _____

Address: _____

City, State, Zip: _____

Telephone: _____

Email address: _____

Cost of books: For orders up to 4 copies, books are $17.95 USD each. For orders of 5 or more books, call (877) 352-9684 or (775) 303-8201.

Sales tax: Please add 7.375% for books shipped to Nevada addresses.

Shipping by U.S. Postal Service:
U.S.: $4.00 for first book and $2.00 for each additional book
International: $9.00 for first book and $5.00 for each additional book

THANK YOU!